"This book is transformational! Being a parent is the hardest job in the world and raising a child with a disability is even harder. This book helped me look at my child through a lens of possibilities versus the limitations that society has placed. I feel empowered and encouraged to create the path that is best suited for what my child needs."

—Tiffany Feingold, Co-Founder and Director of Opportunities at Guiding Bright Minds

"Dr. Winking's stories are so important for educators to read and to share with parents and families. The 12 Habits that she defines will contribute so much to our school communities as we work together to support all students reaching their full potential. Don't miss this book!"

—Rosanne Fulton, PhD, Director of the Center for Urban Education at the University of North Colorado

"A well-researched and empowering reminder that 'difference' does not mean 'deficit,' and that our beliefs and actions shape our children's realities—this book provides a carefully designed formula that every parent can benefit from!"

—Olivia Lindstrom, Co-Founder of Delight Station

of related interest

Raising Kids with Hidden Disabilities
Getting It
Naomi Simmons
ISBN 978 1 83997 155 6
eISBN 978 1 83997 156 3

Autism Abracadabra
Seven Magic Ingredients to Help Develop Your Child's Interactive Attention Span
Kate Wilde
ISBN 978 1 78775 751 6
eISBN 978 1 78775 752 3

Low-Demand Parenting
Dropping Demands, Restoring Calm, and Finding
Connection with your Uniquely Wired Child
Amanda Diekman
ISBN 978 1 83997 768 8
eISBN 978 1 83997 769 5

RAISING
CAPABLE KIDS

The 12 Habits Every Parent Needs Regardless
of their Child's Label or Challenge

Deborah Winking, PhD

Jessica Kingsley Publishers
London and Philadelphia

First published in Great Britain in 2024 by Jessica Kingsley Publishers
An imprint of John Murray Press

1

Copyright © Deborah Winking 2024
Foreword © Gwennyth Palafox 2024

The right of Deborah Winking to be identified as the Author
of the Work has been asserted by her in accordance with
the Copyright, Designs and Patents Act 1988.

Front cover image source: Shutterstock®. The cover image is for
illustrative purposes only, and any person featuring is a model.

A CIP catalogue record for this title is available from the
British Library and the Library of Congress

ISBN 978 1 80501 109 5
eISBN 978 1 80501 110 1

Printed and bound in the United States by Integrated Books International

Jessica Kingsley Publishers' policy is to use papers that are natural,
renewable and recyclable products and made from wood grown in sus-
tainable forests. The logging and manufacturing processes are expected
to conform to the environmental regulations of the country of origin.

Jessica Kingsley Publishers
Carmelite House
50 Victoria Embankment
London EC4Y 0DZ

www.jkp.com

John Murray Press
Part of Hodder & Stoughton Limited
An Hachette Company

For Jeanette—
1931–2023

You raised each one of us to believe that we "could do anything we put our minds to" and we believed you.

Contents

*Foreword by Dr. Gwennyth Palafox,
Clinical Psychologist*   9

Introduction: Raising a Capable Kid Regardless
of Challenge or Diagnosis   11

Habit #1   Believe that Effort Creates Ability   33

Habit #2   Listen to Your Child: Lean into Their
Natural Curiosities to Build Agency and Skills,
and Have Fun   49

Habit #3   Set a Vision of Capable with Your Child
and Adjust It over Time   65

Habit #4   Put the Diagnosis in Its Place, Your Child Is
a Kid First.   81

Habit #5   Name Your Fears and Use Your Vision of Capable
to Help Tame Them   107

Habit #6   Send Capable Messages: Use Words and Act in
Ways that Let Your Child Know that You Think
They Are Capable.   125

Habit #7   Set the Expectation that Others Treat Your Child
as Capable 135

Habit #8   Challenge Your Child (with Support) in Ways
that Regularly Take Them (and You) Outside
Your Comfort Zone 147

Habit #9   Walk Alongside Professionals to Help Your
Child Learn How They Learn Best and Get
Them the Support and Services They Need 161

Habit #10 Allow Your Child to Make Choices and
Experience the Consequences of Those Choices.... 191

Habit #11 Celebrate Your Child's Persistence to Build a
Narrative of Strength 207

Habit #12 Treat Yourself with Compassion, Make Mistakes,
Laugh, and Learn from Them 217

            *Epilogue: Affiliation, Friendship, and
Relationships* 238

APPENDICES: CAPABLE PARENTING HABIT GUIDES 241

            Suggested Reading............................... 254

            References....................................... 255

Foreword

Dr. Gwennyth Palafox, Clinical Psychologist

Parenting books are everywhere, but few resonate as compassionately, insightfully, and empoweringly as *Raising Capable Kids* by Dr. Deborah Winking. As a psychologist who has supported the neurodivergent community for decades, Dr. Winking has emerged as a beacon of guidance for parents navigating the unique journey of raising neurodivergent children of all ages. My absolute favorite thing about Dr. Winking? She unabashedly, wholeheartedly, firmly, and deeply believes that neurodivergent children are capable and she wants everyone to get on board with this message.

In this book, Dr. Winking builds upon the foundation she so vulnerably laid in her previous book, *Capable: A Story of Triumph for Children the World Has Judged as "Different."* With a delicate blend of her experiences as a mother, teacher, and researcher, Dr. Winking weaves together stories of families who are raising neurodivergent children to highlight 12 Habits that parents need to get into their wheelhouse in order to raise children who are not only capable, but children who believe that they are capable of living a life with meaning, purpose, joy, and fulfillment.

This book is not just a to do list or a collection of theories, but rather an invitation for parental transformation. Through storytelling and teaching with concrete steps and examples, the book focuses on the everyday attitudes and actions that bridge the gap between the good intentions that parents have and the lived reality of parenting neurodivergent children. As Dr. Winking proposes in her book, children are nurtured in homes where they are treated as capable, putting the responsibility of raising capable children in the hands of parents. This book guides parents to reflect on their beliefs and implicit assumptions, to challenge societal norms, and to understand, embrace, and accept their children for who they are and the belief that their children are capable. Her teaching expertise shines through as she promotes bite-sized change that is accessible to all.

I will be recommending this book to my clients and anyone who will listen. The habits that Dr. Winking promotes are mindset and attitude shifts that not only families but our world needs. Part parenting guide and part social disrupter, *Raising Capable Kids* dares us to create environments that challenge ableism, promote acceptance and compassion, and to see people for their strengths and talents instead of their deficits. May this book be a source of guidance, inspiration, and action call to create places where neurodivergent children of all ages feel understood, seen, and celebrated. It is with this sense of genuine belonging where positive change happens for all.

Introduction

RAISING A CAPABLE KID REGARDLESS OF CHALLENGE OR DIAGNOSIS

I thought I said all I had to say in my previous book *Capable*.[1] My very personal parenting saga was the book I wanted to write. I love stories. They have captivated me since I was a kid. When under their spell, you assume you are just being entertained until you realize that all along you have been learning something about yourself without even trying. For my money there is no better teacher. I set out to use "story" to give readers a visceral sense of what it is like to raise a child to be capable in the midst of the "mess." Because that glorious, exhilarating, confounding mess is precisely where we parents find ourselves.

Each of us lovingly and somewhat naively signs on to be the ringmaster of our own stunningly complex three (or four or more) ring circus. We are the masters of choreography across all the rings; giving each of our little "acts" the precise degree of love and support they need to shine in the arena in which they are performing, while still sustaining, encouraging, and promoting the acts that are underway simultaneously within all the other rings. We ringmasters transcend the rings while being inextricably connected to each of them. We survey and conduct the action from a distance, while we are, at the same time, every bit a part of the circus, bringing our own personal history of performance highs and lows with us under the big top.

....

1   *Capable: A Story of Triumph for Children the World Has Judged as "Different"* (High Expectations Press, 2021).

Mind bogglingly, we are called to do all of this with a smile on our faces while juggling multiple roles and keeping all balls in the air—because after all, the show must go on!

You may smile at the chaos implied in this plate-spinning, clown-car-riding, parenting metaphor. But in fact, our real-life family systems are more complicated than anything Messrs Barnum or Bailey could dream up. Because while a performance has a definite beginning and end, parenting is a life's work. It can be a tightrope walk on the best of days, and it is made exponentially more demanding when our child has been given a label or diagnosis marking them as somehow "not measuring up."

THE POWER OF STORY...

Since before the written word, humans have been using storytelling to pass lessons down through generations. I too hoped to teach through my story. My conceit was that in the process of reading *Capable* parents would move along parallel tracks. On the surface is the circuitous tale of raising Jack, a boy born with a rare genetic syndrome from birth to adulthood. Underneath is the stream of consciousness describing my headspace and the choices that governed the million and one parenting decisions and micro-decisions that led to the opportunities and limits which became Jack's lived experience.

Riding these two rails together the reader would become swept up in Jack's story while also learning something about their own situation. They would find themselves rooting for Jack to prevail over a system that was designed to sort and toss him into the bin labeled "less than." At the same time the story would coax readers to step out of our world and imagine a path for themselves. A path that would help their own child succeed—whatever his challenges may be. A new genre, "a teaching memoir," was what I optimistically hoped for. Readers would find not only a level of justice for Jack and his mom, but to the extent that they could place themselves in the story, they would seek its counsel and use it as a roadmap for their own parenting journey. I was looking for a "she-did-it-with-her-kid-and-maybe-I-could-do-it-too" kind of vibe.

...AND ITS LIMITATIONS

Unfortunately the very thing that makes a memoir perfect is also its Achilles heel. *Capable* is uniquely my story. As such, it is true, honest, and inscrutable—for me. No one can argue with that. It engages and carries authority because it happened. Its punch lies in the real experiences it relates. But no matter its ability to seduce and immerse readers, the memoir's strength is ultimately also its kryptonite; it is, in the end, only one story. Generous social scientists would call it a "case study" of sorts, a qualitative investigation with an "*N* of 1." It holds ultimate authority and validity for itself, and maybe others to the extent that they share the specific circumstances of the case.

A beloved reader told me she was entranced by *Capable* and yet was equally bothered by its eccentricities. "Great, it worked out for you, you are a special education teacher with a string of letters behind your name, and what appears from the book to be eternal optimism and boundless energy. What about the rest of us?" Fair question. I will let it lie like the proverbial sleeping dog for the moment, but I promise to return to it.

The memoir has a second drawback. My story is powerful (I hope) in its honesty, humanness, gnawing sadness, unshakable hopefulness, and relatable humor. In *Capable*, I share my doubts, missteps, false starts, and harsh critique. My inner monologue is the glue that binds this true story. But it is not research. It does not advance new theories through qualitative or quantitative methods. It does not validate a path forward by triangulating experiences across multiple cases. It is just my story. I make a lot of mistakes and have come to wear those mistakes like a badge of honor. "Let those parents among us who haven't erred cast the first stone."

I engage in more than a little "self-stoning" in *Capable*. I question my quest for "typical" and condemn my preoccupation with Jack passing as "normal" (whatever that is), while at the same time inexplicably wishing it for my child. I put my kid through unnecessary tests in hopes of proving potential critics wrong, instead of just letting him be and celebrating his uniqueness. In those instances, I risked giving my child the message that he was not okay just as he was. I did all of this even as I preached the power of the messages that parents send their kids. How's that for vulnerability, Brené Brown?

I feel immense gratitude that my honest intention for the book broke through, and in large part rose above my parental shortcomings and miscalculations (read humanness). I take heart from scores of readers who offered comments like "After reading this book I will never allow others to treat my son as disabled," "Dr Winking's story has helped me see and nurture 'possibility' in my child," "We now have a path forward," "I now recognize that my child is so much more than her label," etc.

Like I said, *Capable* was the book I wanted to write, relatable and compelling, real and human. It showcases the mistakes I made—the book is littered with them. Memoirs tell stories, recount experiences. *Capable* tells my parenting story warts and all. Readers hear me agonize over choices and question myself throughout the book. There is an unattributed saying: Sometimes you win, sometimes you learn. I know there was learning in my mistakes. However, on balance, *Capable* remains a true story, not a research-based guide. While I attempt to distill some hard-won lessons, it in no way provides a dependable guide for the millions of parents who are currently juggling as fast as they can under their own big tops.

A SHOOT SPRINGS FORTH

I am happy for the validation and inspiration that *Capable* has offered so many families. But from it erupted a nagging itch that could only be satisfied with a thorough scratching. I was haunted by the words of that wise and disquieted reader: "Great, it worked out for you, you are a special education teacher with a string of letters behind your name, and...eternal optimism and boundless energy."

That itch blossomed into a lingering rash that resided deep under my skin. It is with no false modesty that I say I believe there is nothing special about me. True, I had spent more years in school than is advisable and that landed me "letters behind my name" as the reader had commented. But PhD moms stumble just as often as anyone. Evidence, all the false starts, missteps, and downright wrong thinking that I work through in the pages of *Capable*. I am definitely not some once-in-a-generation "child whisperer" parent savant.

Wearing the hats of teacher, administrator, consultant, and researcher, in addition to parent, I had over the years worked in literally hundreds of classrooms and adult service and school-to-work transition programs. I had counseled just as many families of neurodivergent or disabled kids and young adults. I was humbled by their strength and fascinated by their stories. I mulled over the commonalities and differences, turning them over in my head and sorting them into a giant Venn diagram in my brain. (Recall from elementary school those interlocking circles your teacher had you draw to capture what was the same and different about two or more things.)

The overriding similarity that unites all these families is that medical, educational, or psychological experts had assigned each of their children a label or diagnosis pronouncing them as "not measuring up" in some way or another. But then there were the obvious differences: chasmic disparities between the types of labels assigned to these children. Neurodiversity is a mighty big tent. As the well-worn saying goes, "When you have met one person with autism or intellectual disability, or cerebral palsy, or Down syndrome, or ADHD you have met exactly one person."

What stuck with me was that despite gargantuan differences, these parents shared something. Eventually I developed a hypothesis that has become somewhat of an obsession for me. That is: Families with children labeled neurodivergent or disabled are as unique as the wild flowers in a midsummer Colorado mountain meadow, but if those parents are raising their children to be capable, they share some game-changing commonalities.

To test this hypothesis, I would have to do more than nurse those overlapping Venn diagram circles multiplying in my brain. I began interviewing parents of children with all manner of diagnoses and labels (and some that were self-diagnosed as well). I talked with parents of children who had attention challenges, sensory challenges, emotional challenges, intellectual challenges, communication challenges, relational challenges, and behavior challenges. I spent time with parents who were focused on helping their teenager overcome executive functioning challenges to get into higher education; parents who were focused on helping their teenager overcome interoception challenges to get to the bathroom independently; parents who were concerned with their child using the right words; parents who were concerned with their child using eye gaze technology to create the words they could not speak; parents who were helping their child manage their own emotions and those who were helping their child recognize the emotions of others; parents who were encouraging their child to tolerate math homework; and parents who were encouraging their child to tolerate teeth brushing. You get the picture.

Once I got going it was hard to stop. So I haven't. The interviews continue, even beyond this publication. The stories are funny and tragic, magical and heart-rending, and inspiring and sometimes downright baffling. Like award-winning author Katherine Boo (2014) said, "I don't try to fool myself that the stories of individuals themselves are arguments, I just believe that better arguments...get formulated when we know more about ordinary lives."

What I have learned from analyzing parent and child experiences across this rich cache of everyday stories of ordinary lives has become the driving premise of this book.

It is this: All children who have been somehow labeled by our psychological, educational, and medical diagnostic communities are unique individuals. If we were to lay each child's particular combination of strengths and challenges

end to end, the list would span a rainbow. No matter the breadth and depth of differences, there is a single set of mindsets and habits shared by parents who are raising their child to be capable—whatever capable looks like for them.

Analysis of hundreds of hours of interviews are the genesis of the habits. But even that was not enough. We continue to conduct parent and practitioner surveys to further validate, refine, and sharpen them. This body of work has resulted in the 12 Habits of parents who raise capable kids regardless of their challenges.

One-page capable parenting guides for each of the 12 Habits can be found in the Appendices and can be downloaded from www.jkp.com/catalogue/book/9781805011095

WHY HABITS?

Given the algorithms that govern the webisphere, a person of child-bearing age can't scroll online without tripping over some form of parenting advice. The internet is littered with parenting programs, tips, and tricks, the balance of which offers sound counsel for anyone willing to listen. There is "HALT before responding"—determine if your child's behavior is due to Hunger, Anger, Loneliness, or Tiredness, "Take a seat in the balcony"—remove yourself mentally and take a seat when tensions run high so that you can see your child's behavior from outside the action, "Practice 'time ins' instead of 'time outs,'" and the list goes on. All are positive, intuitively pleasing, and have their roots in research.

Why then, with all that information out there, are parents, particularly those with neurodivergent kids, still struggling, exhausted, and beating themselves up? The answer is of course because of how our brains work. Typically, when tensions are running high with our child, we too are dysregulated, exhausted, and just plain not our best selves. In those moments our ancient brains hop into the driver's seat and we slip into ingrained patterns. That is why when your child is dropping to the grocery store floor, an immovable heap, you can't for the life of you remember the parenting advice you read that was supposed to be foolproof. All those solid, smart, and compassionate instructions are sealed away in your cerebral cortex where you can't access them until the situation where they were needed is long past.

We know that in order to change ourselves so that we can raise our child to be capable we need more than sound advice. We need to change us—our habits and the underlying beliefs that support those habits—so that we respond in ways that put our child on a path to their best life.

That is why *Raising Capable Kids* focuses exclusively on habits and mindsets. Does doing the inner work to internalize the Habits mean that our child will never again attach themself to the linoleum floor in he grocery store? No, but it will help you respond instead of react in those moments. You will be able to make sense of such incidents in light of your larger vision of "capable." Perhaps instead of losing your composure (as I have done) or vowing never to enter a public place of business with your child (yep, I've done this one too), you decide the extent to which navigating grocery store etiquette figures into the vision of capable you have built with your child, and depending on its importance, you make a plan for ensuring that future shopping trips become opportunities for growth toward that vision.

THE MAKING OF A HABIT

When we are stressed out, strung out, or just plain out of steam, it is a lose-lose situation with our kid. Even if you want to try something new, the chaos of the moment prevents you from doing so. That is why parenting tips or tricks alone typically don't get the job done. They hold all the answers when you hear them, but you can't call them up when in your time of need.

What we need are mindshifts that create new ways of regularly "being" with our child: aka habits. Simply stated, habits are acquired behavior patterns that we follow regularly until they are involuntary. We should not be surprised that it takes time to create a solid habit— between two and eight months. It is worth the time it takes to build a positive habit. So as James Clear, prominent habits researcher says, "embrace the long slow walk to greatness."

While we should think of creating a habit as a process and not an event, it is true that the more pleasurable the habit, the quicker it is to solidify. It is a heck of a lot easier to embrace a pattern of munching on a bowl of buttery popcorn in front of the TV after dinner than it is to embrace a pattern of celebrating your child's perseverance when their school grades say otherwise.

It takes intentionality to develop a habit, but once it is formed, it hangs around even when we are not trying. That is when habits really pay off, because as they become automatic, your brain is freed up to do other things. Your knee-jerk reaction may have been to pass on new opportunities to avoid the possibility that your child might "fail" or "fall short," but once you have internalized the habits, you see the game-changing importance of sending your child messages that they are capable and begin to automatically consider new opportunities as invitations for growth instead of labeling them as too risky. Habitual automaticity frees up valuable brain space which you can now put to any number of uses, including imagining how your child might be successful.

Habits are behavior patterns, and mindsets are deeply held beliefs; but which comes first? Do we believe our way into behaving? Or do we behave our way into believing? This is an age-old unresolved debate. The best evidence supports that there is no order, but that behavior and beliefs act like two ends of a teeter totter—one pushing on the other.

You don't have to have the ironclad belief that your child is capable for you to use words and behave in ways that send them the message that you think they are.

Beliefs and behaviors exist in a reinforcing cycle. A behavior may strengthen a belief and a belief may cause you to step out and try on a new behavior.

Particularly when raising your neurodivergent or disabled child to be capable, I encourage a "fake it until you make it" attitude when it comes to beliefs and behaviors. The ultimate power is in the message the child gets from the most influential adults in their life. Since it is the message that matters, I tell my child that they can make it across the monkey bars (words) or even spot them on the monkey bars by shadowing their hips with my arms (actions) even before I am 100% sure they can make it across because the strength of my message may cause them to try that much harder. Even if they don't make it all the way across, even if they end up with a grass-stained knee—the point that breaks through loud and clear is "Mom thinks I can."

Similarly, I may allow my child to make a choice about where to do their homework before I am 100% sure that they will make the best choice, because in experiencing the natural consequences of their own choices (possibly getting a poor grade on their homework due to distractions) they get critical practice in flexing their choice-making muscles. This over time strengthens my belief that experiencing the choice-making and consequence-feeling cycle is necessary to developing personal agency within my child.

In these examples and countless others, over and over, beliefs and behaviors act upon one another in ways that lead to large and small decisions that when repeated over time become habits!

THE 12 HABITS ARE FOR EVERYONE

Our first job is just to love them, that is true, and I hope that comes through in each of the Habits. However, love alone is not enough when our child has been labeled. Our naturally wired instincts—whether toward safety, security, comfort, fears for our child or for ourselves—are all seeded in love. But they can cause us to hold on too tight, protect too much, or conversely they can cause us to push too hard, to chase an exhausting array of remedies and even put stock in so-called cures. Yes we are parents, but first we are human. For all these reasons and more the Habits don't come naturally for all of us, all the time.

But, do you have to be an extraordinary person to master the Habits? While some might be more inclined by physiology, personal philosophy, or temperament, these are mindsets and skills that anyone can learn. I liken it to piano playing. If my statuesque, lithe friend with long, slender fingers and I both set out to learn to play the piano, genetically she may reach the keys more naturally and effortlessly, but with commitment and persistence I can learn to play the piano as well as my friend. The same is true with the Habits found in these pages: folks armed with a natural positive attitude, reserves of persistence, and a devil-may-care attitude toward what others think may have an edge, but all of us can learn and internalize the Habits to help our child see themself as capable.

THE MANY FACES OF CAPABLE

When your child has a disability or is neurodivergent, what does it mean to raise them to be "capable"? To answer that question, we first have to tackle what capable is and what it is not.

Capable does *not* mean curing our child. However, let's be honest, who wouldn't like to wave a magic wand and erase all their child's medical, intellectual, physical, psychological, and sensory difficulties? Besides, if that were even remotely possible, you would have already moved heaven and earth to do so. Aside from its improbability, I believe curing misses the point. It centers all our energy on correcting our child as if he or she were the problem, instead of viewing our child as an amazing being who thinks, moves, communicates, and/or behaves differently. Difference is in no way synonymous with "deficit" but should be thought of instead as something to be understood, celebrated, and "mined" to help your child maximize their potential.

Dictionary.com tells us that *capable* is an adjective meaning "having power and ability." Naturally because each of our children is unique and possesses a vast array of strengths and difficulties, what that power and ability looks like varies. I define capable as an individual living a meaning-filled life (determined by them and the people who love them) with the maximum level of autonomy and agency that they can authentically access. That is a mouthful of words, but when we break it down, isn't that really what we hope for all our children—neurotypical and neurodivergent alike: meaning, agency, and autonomy?

Given this definition, there are as many faces of "capable" as there are individual children and families. We rightly carve out what capable looks like for each of us.

Lest this talk of "capable for all" sounds Pollyanna, let me clarify. Parenting, particularly, a child who is neurodivergent or who has a disability is not a Broadway musical where every problem is solved with a song. Perhaps you are among those of us whose child has multiple challenges. Maybe you are finding it difficult to see strengths through an interminable tangle of developmental or neurological issues. Maybe your child's lack of communication triggers overwhelming frustration, which prevents relationships, which results in their social isolation. Or letters on the page scramble as they reach your child's brain, learning lags squash self-confidence, and school task avoidance follows, which creates gaping holes in their academic skills. Or maybe your child's lack of mobility constricts usual childhood exploration, thereby short-circuiting necessary developmental building blocks. Or your child's chronic health issues render everything else a distant second, and life-sustaining safety precautions get in the way of your child freely associating with his peers. All of these are unrelenting, strength-sapping predicaments that would defeat the greatest Marvel superhero. We did not sign up for any of this, yet here we find ourselves.

Regardless of the severity or combination of challenges your child faces, there is a version of capable that exists uniquely for them—a way for them to access meaning and a level of agency in their lives. What capable looks like depends on your child's developmental level and life circumstances. For example, if your child is growing up in Brooklyn, being capable can look like them independently navigating their city using the subway system rather than a car or bicycle. If your child is 13, capable may look like showing an animal at a county fair rather than working as a veterinarian technician at the neighborhood animal shelter.

We get into the specifics of crafting a vision of capable with your child in Habit #3, but the important thing to remember is that capable is for everyone. I worked with a 12-year-old boy for whom capable was choosing when to turn his head to the side to activate a switch which ran a cool wash cloth across his face. I also worked with a teenage girl who used her eye gaze to beckon Alexa to play her favorite music or TikTok videos. There are other young people with disabilities for whom capable looks like choosing a preferred graduate study program, bringing home a regular paycheck from Walmart, being a full participant in family gatherings, selling greeting cards with images they have painted on them, volunteering as a stable tender at a therapeutic ranch, or regularly playing cards with residents at a senior center. All involve agency, choice, and dignity. All are worthy pursuits that signal meaning for the individual, inspire pride in parents, not to mention making the world a better place for us all.

Regardless of where your child is now and the magnitude of the challenges they face, I guarantee you are better off focusing your energy and intention on what *is* possible rather than on deficits. What "capable" looks like specifically for your child lies within this notion of possibility.

CHANGE YOURSELF, NOT YOUR CHILD

If you were hoping for a book about how to change your child, you bought the wrong book. This book is about changing us. It is about developing the complementary mindsets and habits that will allow you to be a more intentional parent so that your child develops into a capable individual.

Raising a child to be capable is not the result of one heroic act. If it were, it would be so much easier. Rather, capable is the sum of thousands of seemingly insignificant decisions, choices, and actions layered over the course of a childhood. We all want to do our best for our kids, and the Habits will help you achieve this.

If you learn the Habits, and practice them regularly, they will *change you* so that you show up for your child in ways that imbue independence, resilience, and agency. The Habits will inform your decision-making, help you set the conditions, and offer opportunities over time that enable your child to "grow" into their version of capable.

However, parenting is an inexact science, as is everything having to do with humans. As important as intentional parenting is, our children are wonderfully autonomous beings, not puppets at the mercy of our strings. They will develop in their own incomparable, asynchronous ways despite all our love and best efforts. However, recognizing that our children will encounter a world which is better at creating catchy slogans and positive memes about neurodivergence and disability than it is at truly celebrating it and creating welcoming spaces, we parents need to do all we can to help our child to thrive— whatever thriving looks like for them.

"NORMAL" SITS SMACK DAB IN THE MIDDLE OF LAKE WOBEGON

Much shade has been thrown at parents when disability advocates or otherwise "enlightened" individuals get even a whiff of an attitude that we want our kid to be "normal." Worse, we do it to ourselves. We feel guilty when even in private moments we wish our child was "normal." We shake our heads to dispel the demon thought from our minds, like it means we don't love the child we have. Instead of flagellating ourselves for even entertaining such thoughts, involuntary as they are, it is more helpful to sort out what we really mean when we think "normal."

Garrison Keillor, beloved storyteller and Minnesota Public Radio host, began every one of his radio programs "with the latest news from Lake Wobegon, our fictional Minnesota town where all the women are strong, all the men are good looking and all the children are above average." His dry humor exposed the wrong-headedness (not to mention mathematical impossibility) of chasing an illusion that is not doable or even desirable when you really get down to it. Lake Wobegon was a comic illusion, an impossible figment and a boring one at that. Who wants to live in a world where everyone is the same?

Similarly, the notion of "normal" is a boring illusion. Nearly 20% of school age children in the United States are labeled as experiencing a disability. Just as many more identify as neurodivergent but are not formally labeled. Traditional "high achievers" are now willing to talk about their challenges. Our valedictorians battle with anxiety, our trophy winners manage their OCD, and some of the most confident appearing among us struggle with eating disorders.

Combine that with all the beautiful eccentricities, maladies, and quirks out there within those who count themselves among the "neurotypical" population and we have officially rendered the term "normal" as utterly meaningless.

Since "normal" is not really a thing, just an unhelpful, stand-in word, what is the prize we are really coveting when we misuse the word? As the parent of more than one child with a diagnosed disability, I can say that I want life to be easier for my children. When our child has a disability or is neurodivergent in ways that get in the way of "doing" life, we imagine that falling somewhere a little closer to the middle of the bell curve would make school, keeping friends, personal hygiene, getting a job, and just about everything go smoother for them.

Of course we love the kid we have, it is insulting for anyone to think otherwise, we just want to take away the pain, confusion, and disappointment. But when we pause to consider the "normal" (again, whatever that is) kids we know, we see that they endure embarrassments, bullying, tantrums, friend problems, learning struggles, emotional fits, social disappointments, trials, and failures. There is pain to be had in all of these.

As a parent who has gone through and now graduated from "I Wanted My Child to be 'Normal' Anonymous," I believe that what we all truly desire is for our child to be happy, strong, and able to handle whatever life throws their way, whether it is from a body that moves differently, brain that thinks differently, or a communication system that gets ideas across differently. So out with wishing for a boring illusion and in with raising capable kids.

WHAT THIS BOOK IS AND IS NOT

Raising Capable Kids is not a self-help book for adults. Nor is it a child discipline or skill-building handbook. It does not directly teach you how to build a foolproof behavior plan, teach communication skills, or improve your child's learning and attention. There are other excellent books for all of these. What it does offer is a guide to the beliefs, habits, intentional decision paths, and actions that will help you raise your child with maximum competence, agency, and independence. To the extent that you make the habits your own, your child's behavior will improve, communication with your child will improve, and you will maximize your child's chances to learn and gain new skills.

WHO THIS BOOK IS FOR

Nearly 20% of school age children in the United States identify as having a disability or as neurodivergent. Writ large, neurodivergence describes people whose brain differences affect how their brain works. That means they have unique strengths and challenges from people whose brains don't work in those exceptional ways. Neurodivergence does not necessarily signal a disability, only a divergence in brain function—hence the name. Divergence in brain functioning only becomes a disability to the extent that differences get in the way of daily functioning. For example, a person with autism who thinks in the form of pictures has some decided advantages in engineering and spatial tasks. A divergence in brain functioning that gets in the way of reading other people's emotions or seeing things from others' perspectives may or may not be a disability depending on the extent to which it gets in the way of success in school or the community.

Given this understanding, neurodivergence and disability touches us all. This book is for you if your child has been labeled as neurodivergent or disabled by the educational, psychological, and medical powers that be. It is for you if someone or some circumstance has put a limitation on your child. Whether a professional has handed down a diagnosis, or a loved one has offered their projection. Or maybe an accident or traumatic event has altered life for your child.

This book is for you if you have been told your child has Down syndrome, attention deficit/hyperactivity disorder (ADHD), autism spectrum disorder, obsessive compulsive disorder (OCD), is deaf or blind, has cerebral palsy, or uses a wheelchair. It is for you if you have been told that your child has a developmental delay, has severe emotional disturbance, is on the "spectrum," has a visual impairment, has multiple disabilities, or has been judged "health impaired." Because it deals with the ways in which our beliefs, behaviors, and fears affect our children, it is for you if your child has chronic anxiety or an eating disorder that makes you likely to transfer your fears on to your child.

This book is also for you if your child does not have a formal label, but struggles with learning, sensory integration, communication, mobility, or behavior.

Some have argued that this book is for you even if your child is "typically" developing and going through oppositional teen years, certainly a fear-inducing time for us all. Every child, whether neurodivergent or neurotypical, is on their own path, learning in fits and starts, and is subject to circumstantial challenges like divorce, death in the family, incarceration of loved ones, poverty, and housing instability, all of which can cause emotional instability and trauma. Given this modern reality, some hold that all children have special needs and so this book is for parents of all children including those in the general education population.

I agree with the presumption that at some point in the process of growing up, adverse experiences and just life itself may result in any child "presenting" with a special need that impacts learning, relationships, or emotional stability. I personally worked with bright-eyed Brooklyn third-grader Hakem who transformed from model student to multiple behavioral outbursts a day as a result of a messy divorce and home life struggles. During that time, though by all accounts "neurotypical," he required a therapist, behavior analyst, and special education teacher support.

While these situations occur and often leave trauma in their wake, I distinguish relatively short-term circumstantial "special needs" from children who have been diagnosed and labeled by the system or who have had ongoing developmental delays in learning, self-regulation, communication, behavior, and movement. Just the fact of being marked as "different" creates its own trauma and lived ecosystem that is different from that of children generally considered neurotypical.

Because raising a child who has been labeled presents unique complexity, grief, and challenge, I consider these parents my main audience and the focus of my examples and elaboration. To address this vast diversity within the neurodivergent and disability communities, I attempt to offer examples and anecdotes that represent the range, understanding that I will always fall short.

Even though this book does not include scenarios featuring children considered neurotypical, it is true that the Habits are universal and to a large extent apply to all parents.

A ROSE BY ANY OTHER NAME...

Language can trip us up. We "normies" are finally beginning to wise up and listen to the voices of those who are neurodivergent and experience disability. As we do, we are learning a lot about how people see themselves. Over the years disability-first language—"Down syndrome person," "crippled person," etc.—came to be considered archaic and even insulting because it equated a complex individual with a condition and so was replaced with person-first language—"person with an intellectual impairment," "person who uses a wheelchair," etc. However, sensibilities are always shifting and leaders today, particularly in the autistic community, see autism not as "a condition that they have" but as who they are and so prefer the terms "autistic person," "he is autistic." Ultimately, being addressed using person-first language or disability-first language should be determined by the individual. Both are equally valid depending on how one identifies. I respect both and so intentionally use person-first and disability-first language throughout these pages.

MAKING IT EASY

Raising capable kids is all about harnessing a parent's second greatest superpower in service of our child. Why focus on seconds you ask?

Our greatest parental superpower, hands down, is love, and that is something that can't be taught. But our second greatest superpower is intentionality. Here there is room for growth for us all. We parents show what matters to us by what we pay attention to, and what we pay attention to gets done.

With this in mind I encourage you to be intentional in consuming the Habits. While "parent" is undoubtedly our most important job title, it is rarely our only one. We are also "employees," "bosses," "housekeepers," "yard maintenance workers," and "caretakers for aging parents," just to name a few. Parents with a child with a disability are so busy, we are lucky if we get through the day without forgetting a dose of medication, missing a therapy appointment, or losing our composure with our child. Where is the time or brain power for intentionality? We survive on muscle memory and smartphone reminders.

Because I have been there, a working mom of four children, I strive to present the Habits in a way that is easy to digest. I have purposefully kept jargon to a minimum and only resort to education-ese when it is absolutely necessary. I use real-life stories and examples to bring each Habit to life. Each Habit stands on its own and can be considered individually. But they are also interrelated and rooted in a common mindset, and as such they work best together to help you make decisions, behave, and be with your child in ways that grow competence and agency over time. Once you make the Habits your own, you will feel more confident in your parenting and, perhaps even more importantly, you will enjoy life with your child more.

For each Habit you first get a glimpse of it in the form of a short story showcasing the Habit in action. These are all real-life stories curated from amazing, courageous, flawed individuals who are parenting their own child with particular strengths and challenges (aka regular families just like yours). In telling the stories, I have intentionally not included the child's label or diagnosis, because the label itself is not the point. I don't want the diagnosis to conjure stereotypical images, dominate, or distract readers from the central message of the stories.

In doing so I am being true to my belief that any diagnosis only describes part of a complex individual who possesses a multitude of interests, passions, and proclivities. It is like if I wanted to tell a story about my considerable struggles learning to play pickleball and I led with my diagnosis of bladder exstrophy. My bladder exstrophy, diagnosed at birth, plays a part in the story because it led to a good deal of childhood trauma and explains my frequent trips to the bathroom that interrupt the game and why I don't drink water on the court. But equally important facts in this story are that I am an uber-extrovert, who enjoys competition, has never played sports, and that my exuberance outpaces my poise in all athletic pursuits.

It is true that many of our children's diagnoses have monumental impact on their lives, but I choose to talk about them in terms of their practical impacts rather than leading with a diagnostic label which carries its own baggage. I wanted readers to relate to the children and young adults in the stories for their humanness—e.g., individuals who love music, prefer to be alone, are extremely creative, overly rely on their technology (aka all kids), are jokers, are opinionated, or who avoid unfamiliar experiences rather than be eclipsed by a diagnosis that flattens and stereotypes them. However, at the same time I recognize that as a parent looking for a path forward, the diagnosis or educational label is enlightening, so I have referenced specific diagnoses for each story in the footnotes.

To help readers understand the "why" behind the Habit, I offer a brief explanation of the neuroscience that underlies each. A working understanding of the science is particularly useful because it makes a compelling case for the power behind each Habit and why it is important for parents to pursue each one. I have tried to tread lightly on the science so as not to drown out the message in scholarly discourse. Some references are included for readers who want to delve further into the research base behind each of the Habits.

In addition to other families' experiences, I often include a vignette or anecdote from raising Jack, that connects back to *Capable*. I hope that readers might find this connection with the first book and the author's personal experience desirable.

TAKE BITE-SIZED ACTION

The Habits will ensure that you raise a capable child regardless of their challenges, but *only* if you learn, practice, and internalize them. However don't expect to master them all at once, and don't beat yourself up if it takes time.

Bite-sized actions, layered on one another, that is how all change happens. Little shifts, imperceptible at first and then larger. Maybe you begin thinking about "what is" and "what is possible" for your child. Then you find yourself taking notice of how their special interest, no matter how idiosyncratic, calms or builds confidence. Next thing you know you are acting, pausing before you accept a new service or support for your child instead of blindly accepting it. And before you know it you are regularly using the vision of capable you have developed with your child to determine the opportunities you make sure he or she is able to access.

Our brains can't learn when we are stressed. It is important to think on and practice the habits in relaxed moments when the stakes are not high. The reflection questions at the end of each Habit section are carefully designed to help you turn a mirror on your own thoughts and behaviors. Not always easy, it is okay if you are not where you want to be in terms of seeing your child as capable. None of us are. I worked with a couple who swore they were communicating to their child that he was capable, until they considered all the things they were avoiding, like allowing him to opt out of contributing to family meals, planning for family outings without him, getting his Father's Day gifts for him, etc.

Don't gloss over these questions. I advise using a journal or your phone to capture your thinking.

The best way to get comfortable with new beliefs and behaviors is to dip a toe in. The Try It On exercises allow you to do just that. This is how you begin making the Habits how you "do life" with your child. It takes a village is actually wise counsel. Join other parents and family members in consuming the Habits, even consider serving as accountability partners for one another.

A WORD TO SEND YOU ON YOUR WAY

Start with the end in mind. I have ordered the Habits 1–12, but I suggest starting with Habit #12 first: Treat Yourself with Compassion, Make Mistakes, Laugh, and Learn from Them. Because we have to address how we treat ourselves in order to embrace and internalize the remaining Habits. It is only by getting right with ourselves that we can show up for our child.

Regardless of your child's current functioning level I invite you to focus not on what *is* but what *is possible* for your child. I share the Habits in the hope that my experiences and the experiences of others are instructive. The Habits are game-changing, but it is also true that there are no quick fixes. Parenting is a game of inches. Let the Habits and stories that underlie them serve as an inspiration to transform what you think and how you respond to your child day in and day out, so that over time they get the all-important message that they are "capable."

Believe that Effort Creates Ability

ADIOS, LITTLE FRIEND

"Every day, a gift." That is how Melanie marked the time with Samuel through an infancy marked more by seizures than smiles. She had lost count of the number of times she had to resuscitate him. Alarmingly frequent bursts of electrical activity were hammering away at precious cells and neural connections, slowly killing her son.

With no way to control or reduce the intensity of the seizures, the draconian "Hail Mary" doctors offered was to remove the seizure focal point in Samuel's brain. After months of testing, surgeons successfully removed most of the left temporal lobe. The prognosis was consistent across the surgeon, neurologist, and epileptologist: "The boy is alive but don't expect him to walk or talk, since these regions of the brain no longer exist."

Post-surgery, Melanie drank in the vision of her sleeping baby, brain and limbs coexisting in harmonious stillness. She welcomed this new son, neither totally convinced of the experts' dire prognosis nor hopeful—just content, counting this second birth as "Day 1 for Samuel."

As he grew, Melanie took advantage of every type of occupational and physical therapy available. Over time the boy actually began propelling himself around the house in a device called a gait trainer equipped with steel bars that protected him on all sides. At age five, Samuel, accompanied by his mom and encased in his protective steel pod, navigated, albeit lurchingly, into the epileptologist's office. It was at that moment that the elderly specialist revised his earlier diagnosis for all in "waiting room-range" to hear. He exclaimed with an exuberance Melanie did not think the old doc had in him, "The boy will walk! The boy will walk!"

Despite this victory, the balance of Samuel's days was spent in his wheelchair. Encouraged by the possibilities that her son's spasmodic movement held, Melanie decided that the wheelchair would become a tool for walking, not sitting. Soon every errand became yet another opportunity for Samuel not to ride but to push the wheelchair—nicknamed his "little friend"—a helper who was there by his side only if Samuel needed him.

Epic mother–son battles ensued in the wide aisles of Walmart each time Samuel collapsed onto the parquet floors in protest—his way of communicating that he strongly preferred the comfort of the ride to moving his own limbs against gravity. Melanie ignored alarmed shoppers who unwittingly had a front row seat to the drama. She pulled out every trick in the book to get Samuel behind the chair instead of in it—including bribery. "Samuel, if we walk, we can get ice cream…no stopping or dropping allowed." She braved Samuel's and her own tears as she coaxed him up again and again to propel his "little friend" onward.

Years later Melanie had occasion to wipe more tears from her eyes, but this time they were tears of joy, as she watched Samuel, now a teenager, climb onto the bus and walk to his seat, his "little friend" discarded.

While speech has not come yet for Samuel, today he moves through the world on his own two feet. And so it came to pass that the boy who experts considered "not a candidate for mobility" walks. These days, Samuel saves his "rides" for roller coasters at amusement parks.[1]

The Habit: Capable parents and caregivers believe to their core that

1 Samuel is diagnosed with intractable epilepsy and global developmental delays.

ability is fluid, not fixed, and that intentional effort applied over time can expand their child's aptitude.

This powerful belief is the raw material that fuels all manner of possibility. Said simply, none of us, your child included, is stuck with the hand they were dealt. Think of it as merely a starting point.

It is true that for our children with disabilities "effort" often includes additional support, scaffolds, and work-arounds. However, the fact remains that almost every human function from mobility to moderating feelings to math computation has the capacity to grow and change through intentional effort.

Most of us, if asked, would say, of course, we believe our ability is not fixed and that, aside from the freak lottery ticket or serendipitous chance encounter, we create our futures largely through our own volition. Here's the catch, unfortunately, for our children with a disability, there is something about the formality and finality of the diagnosis or label—applied with medical, psychological, and educational precision—that causes us pause. It makes us question this idea that we accept as a matter of course for ourselves and for our neurotypical children.

Believing that effort generates potential does not discount the very real challenges that our children face. The obstacles that neurodivergent children or those with disabilities face are famously more severe, pernicious, and enduring than that of their neurotypical peers. In fact, difficulty is actually baked into the sauce. The word *disability* literally means "without ability." No wonder we are skeptical of a belief that says ability is malleable and can improve for kids who have been stamped *disabled.*

Capable parents do not allow the label, diagnosis, or even their child's current behavior to shake their belief that effort creates ability and this belief leads to a limitless stream of everyday decisions and behaviors that create otherwise unimaginable possibilities for our children.

THE SCIENCE BEHIND THE HABIT

No one would give "natural ability" the credit for Samuel proudly stepping aboard that school bus. It was sustained effort that literally exploded his walking "aptitude" or potential over time. Through repetition and practice, other regions of Samuel's brain took up the mobility function that was native to the now nonexistent left temporal lobe.

Ability is not fixed, rather it is what we do every day, each little microdecision, whether it be to take on something new or "sit this one out," that fuels aptitude within us all. Each and every decision that leads to tackling a new task for the first time, trying another way when things don't work out, or repeating a sequence of steps over and over works to etch new neural pathways within our brains, expanding our repertoire of behavior. The scientific term for this is neuroplasticity. But it all starts with a belief—something we hold to be true and so act upon it.

In fact, we don't just win or lose in some great cosmic lottery. While it is true enough that some of us are born with greater quantities of raw material than others, in the end our ability is molded by what we *do*. A six-foot-three-inch-tall young woman who has been graced with long, lithe arms and legs has a genetic edge in making the college basketball team, but with hard work and determination other players well short of six foot can become just as valued on the team.

The notion that "effort creates aptitude," an educational concept pioneered at the University of Pennsylvania's Learning Research Development Center (Resnick 1995), was like a bucket of cold water in the face of an international intelligence testing apparatus that purported to measure a person's aptitude as a fixed quantity. Simply put, "effort creates aptitude" means that what you *put in* determines what you *get out*. Despite the fact that the grandfather of intelligence testing himself, Alfred Binet, believed in fluid ability and resisted quantifying intelligence as a static quality, over time IQ testing became synonymous with "measuring" ability. In fact, as recently as the 1990s, books like *The Bell Curve* (Herrnstein and Murray 1994) laid out a case that intelligence is largely fixed and does not change measurably over the lifespan.

Newer research-based powerhouse books like *Mindset* (Dweck 2007) and *Grit* (Duckworth 2018) have popularized the idea underlying the science that what we believe about what we can do matters more than a number on a test. They show that a fixed mindset (believing that you are either good at something or not) is a learning and effort killer; and that a growth mindset (believing that you can get better with effort) actually tips the scale and improves performance in positive ways. Much has been made of the virtues of a growth mindset. This research has given birth to catchy sayings and handy bromides that are the stuff of trending online memes: "We fail forward"; "Whether you believe you can or you believe you can't you are right"; "Edison discovered 999 ways not to create a light bulb"; "If you believe you can't learn, no one can help you. If you believe you can learn, no one can stop you"; and the list goes on.

The decorative inspirational sign market ballooned with the growth of mindset research. But in fact *Mindset* author Carol Dweck states that in truth most people are not purely growth or fixed in their thinking, but a mix of both. Importantly, the view you adopt for yourself profoundly affects the way you lead your life.

The fact is we are drawn to these research-inspired memes because they connect us to a relentless positivity that we want to be true. But to be clear, in order to raise our child with a disability as capable, positivity itself is not enough. We must *act* in ways that create potential-building opportunities.

This Habit is made up of two parts:

- *The belief.* We believe that all humans can change, that we and our children can do better.

- *The behavior.* We act on this belief with thoughts and decisions that prompt behaviors which provide children with opportunities to change and grow.

APPLYING THE HABIT

The power of B²: Beliefs and behavior working together

Beliefs and behavior that reinforce each other are a powerhouse for creating change. Let's take a look at how these two work together to create opportunities for your child.

First we have to believe that we and our children can do better. But, as we said, belief is not enough, these beliefs must lead to thoughts and decisions that prompt tangible actions. What specifically do these "behaviors" look like in parents and children? Parents provide ongoing opportunities, give of their time, create space in the day for their child to learn, encourage their child to try, and identify and enlist therapies, alternatives, and supports. Children try new things, engage in practice and repetition, re-engage after taking breaks, persist through errors, and try another way when the learning curve is steep.

For Melanie, believing, hoping, and wishful thinking alone did not cause Samuel to "pick up his mat and walk" (to borrow a proverbial phrase), or in this case to "discard his wheelchair and walk." However, Melanie believed that her son's ability was not fixed, and that absent uncontrolled seizures Samuel could change and grow, despite medical prognoses to the contrary. That core belief acted upon all of the decisions Melanie made and the behaviors that followed. This cocktail of beliefs and intentional behaviors interacting on one another over time created potential. The compounding weight and repetition of those microdecisions and individual behaviors made every day and over time fueled the change in aptitude in Samuel.

Let's double click on the thoughts, decisions, and behavior part of the habit. The belief changed what Melanie thought was possible. Those thoughts affected the decisions Melanie made and the rational behaviors that followed which provided Samuel with opportunities that increased his potential for walking over the long run. Seeing her son first nudge his weight against the wall of the gait trainer made her believe that the way he moved could change—she did not know by how much, but that potential was there.

Melanie's belief: Absent uncontrolled seizures, Samuel's ability to move may change, I saw him move in the gait trainer despite medical prognoses to the contrary.

Belief prompted Melanie's *thoughts and decisions:*

- The portion of the day that Samuel sat in the wheelchair needed to decrease.

- Time spent in the wheelchair was getting in the way of him moving.

- Pushing the empty wheelchair while holding on to the back of the headrest for balance was one safe way to increase movement.

- Her worries that other people might see her son struggling when he was pushing the wheelchair were not helpful to getting her son moving.

- Spending time feeling sad and afraid about how difficult walking was for Samuel got in the way of her encouraging movement.

- Focusing on the next steps he would take, where he would take them, and the confidence that those next steps would give her son helped her encourage movement.

These *thoughts and decisions* led to a pattern of *behavior* on Melanie's part:

- She sought out places where Samuel would be motivated to push his wheelchair.

- She included Samuel on errands that presented opportunities to push instead of leaving him home.

- She dismissed the glances and indignant stares of onlookers.

- She came up with and used upbeat one liners that acted like a salve on concerned bystanders. "You know how stubborn tweens can be," "We are taking turns pushing and it is his turn," "Don't we all feel this way after a hard day!" etc.

- She praised and rewarded Samuel's attempts at walking.

- She "talked up" walking as something desirable and expected with him and with others. "I love how you are walking," "My son walked all the way through the toy section at Target today," etc.

Melanie's belief that Samuel's movement could improve led to thoughts and decisions that prompted concrete behaviors, which provided Samuel with abundant opportunities to increase his aptitude for movement and ultimately walking.

This is the B² formula:

Beliefs lead to **thoughts and decisions** that prompt **behaviors** which provide **opportunities** for **change** and **growth** that etch new neural pathways within the brain.

The reverse is also true

Melanie had a growth mindset. But it is important to note that this formula works no matter if the belief reflects a fixed or growth mindset. Imagine the reverse—if Melanie believed unwaveringly in what the surgeons, neurologists, and epileptologists foretold: Samuel did not have the ability to walk because of the removal of his left temporal lobe, the portion associated with movement. This belief would have been reasonable given the circumstances and, no doubt, would have led to a very different sequence of thoughts, decisions, and behaviors, which would have resulted in different opportunities for Samuel.

The *belief*: Because of the surgery removing the portion of Samuel's brain that governs walking, he does not have the ability to walk. That ability is not likely to change much.

This belief could reasonably lead to the following *thoughts and decisions*:

- Time spent focusing on walking gets in the way of other positive experiences Samuel could be having.

- Focusing on something that he can't do agitates Samuel and tires him out, creating less time to learn other things.

- Focusing on walking makes Samuel the focus of other people's attention. That attention whether negative or positive puts pressure on Samuel.

- I don't like how I feel when I require Samuel to do something that is so hard for him and which is unlikely to make a difference.

- We need to make movement and transitions as easy as possible for Samuel and the caregivers who support him.

- The less time caregivers have to spend pushing and transferring Samuel in his chair, the more they can spend focusing on learning other important skills and concepts.

These *thoughts and decisions* could have reasonably led to the following patterns of *behavior* on Melanie's part:

- She gets a bigger and more comfortable wheelchair.

- She gets a motorized wheelchair that simplifies mobility for Samuel and his caregivers.

- She chooses to include Samuel only on errands where he can participate sitting in this chair and where taking his chair is not too unwieldy.

- She opts out of including him on outings to sandy and rocky areas where the chair won't roll easily.

- She involves him in activities where moving one's legs is not central (e.g., music therapy, art therapy, movie nights, pizza parties, etc.).

- She deemphasizes the importance of walking as a way of getting around when talking with Samuel and when talking about Samuel to others.

All these decisions decrease opportunities for repetition and movement practice, while increasing opportunities for activities that Samuel can do in his chair. Samuel's aptitude for movement stays about the same, he remains in his wheelchair, while potentially gaining other skills that do not have to do with movement or walking.

A marathon, not a sprint

Like most worthwhile accomplishments in life, the effort-creates-ability habit does not impact performance overnight. This is how the beliefs–decisions–behaviors formula played out over time for Samuel. At two-and-a-half years old his aptitude for movement was nil. The region of the brain assigned to movement was missing and he displayed no signs of potential. With effort and over time his aptitude increased from relying on the gait trainer that stabilized his core and did much of the work for him, to pushing a wheelchair while using it for balance, to finally walking independently, only occasionally needing assistance.

Ever heard the old adage "He showed no signs of aptitude for..."? Why is the word "show" so often linked in phraseology with the notion of aptitude? Because aptitude is often signaled by what is visible and what can be measured. The very idea of aptitude as something that is "shown" indicates its fluidity and perhaps also the complex relationship between aptitude, interest, and motivation. For example, I am not showing much aptitude for tennis right now because at the moment I am more interested in running, so I am not out there swinging my tennis racket.

It is impossible to calculate the role of interest and motivation in increasing ability. Our story may have ended very differently if Samuel had no interest in moving. But he did, as evidenced by him nudging his bodyweight against the gait trainer. Melanie, for her part, took full advantage of that interest, which likely intensified as he increasingly received his mom's and others' positive feedback and rewards whenever he moved.

It is equally important to note that verbal communication, another function governed by the absent portion of Samuel's brain, has not developed (so far). Reminding us that beliefs do not and cannot cure. What they do is set in motion precious opportunities for change. Even if our belief is not fully realized, our child ends up in a better place for the act of trying. Melanie says that the effort would have been worth it for the core strength and stamina Samuel has gained, even if he stopped short of fully discarding his wheelchair.

Most of us can picture that teacher that we recall fondly because they made us believe in ourselves or love science, or who is the reason we are in the profession we are today. Conversely, we remember the teacher, coach, or elder who told us we could not sing, led us to believe that we should not bother trying out for the track team, or that writing was just "not our cup of tea." Founder of Research for Better Teaching Jon Saphier encourages teachers to believe in their students: "Smart is something you get, not something you are born with" (Saphier 2016).

This premise extends not just to "smarts" but to ability writ large, and includes all manner of capabilities: strength, voice, social skills, confidence, balance, to name a few.

The power and peril of belief

Reader, if you are a skeptic, now is the appropriate time to ask: "Come on, how much can our beliefs about a person actually change their behavior?" Believing my child can fly will not make him a pilot. If my child has Down syndrome, I can believe in him until the cows come home and it will not create a new chromosomal chain. If he is paralyzed due to a severed spinal cord, my beliefs will not mend neural connections, bone, and ligaments. This is true. Beliefs themselves do not cure and we are not in the business of faith healing.

The notion of "curing" misses the point and implies that our children are the problem, are wrong, somehow defective.

However, we parents *are* in the business of helping our child live his or her best life given the very real challenges they face. Within autism, deaf, and many other ability communities, there is a sustained movement that reminds us all that difference should not be confused with "deficit." Autism spectrum disorder advocates point out that the autistic brain does not think *wrong*, it merely thinks *differently*. The deaf community has shown the world that vocal communication is only one way of getting one's point across and is not innately superior to sign language.

We love our children for all their exquisite uniqueness. We want them to live meaningful lives, while embracing their uniqueness, and at the same time, we want them never to be constrained by negative beliefs, feelings of helplessness, or limited by fear.

We will not "wish" or "hope" our child into walking, talking, speaking without a stutter, reading fluently, learning math, recognizing others' emotions, or being able to focus on school work. Habit #1 requires that parents believe that ability is fluid, regardless of the raw material our child starts with, and then requires them to focus on the specific thoughts, decisions, and behaviors that accompany that belief.

How much can be achieved through thoughts, decisions, and behaviors, sown over the totality of a young lifetime, that reflect a belief that our child *can*? It turns out, *a lot*. Leading mindset researchers are proving that the possibilities are expanding as we learn more about how particular beliefs impact outcomes: "as we understand how one person affects another person, the line of what is possible can actually move" (Dweck 2007).

What could happen for our children if we believed in them and their innate capacity to achieve despite the labels pronounced over them?

What we believe about our child impacts our thoughts, the decisions we make, and our behavior toward them. If we *believe* our kids are bright and capable, we will make decisions which lead to behaviors that provide them with opportunities to expand their aptitude. This equation will not "cure" our child, but it will give them the best chance of expanding and fulfilling their potential.

REFLECT...

- Dig deep. What do I really believe about my child's potential? What decisions have these beliefs caused? How do I support or limit my child with my beliefs?

- How does what I believe shape the thoughts I have, the parenting decisions I make, and the opportunities I offer my child?

- Do I believe that deliberate practice, exposure, and repeated opportunities will result in growth over time? Do I have evidence of this in my own life?

- What is one thing my child has achieved (or is in the process of achieving)? How did it happen or how is it happening?

- Do I believe that my child has the potential to _____ (fill in the blank), learn, attend, read, walk, use a communication device, communicate verbally or nonverbally, go to college, join in at birthday parties, etc.?

- What behaviors or expressions of interest no matter how small have I seen within my child that makes me think they *can* _____?

- How does what I see in my child confirm or contradict my child's label, diagnosis, or expert prognoses?

TRY IT ON...

- Write in a journal or speak notes into your phone to keep track of the thoughts you have about your child's potential for growth. Note your child's expressions of interest no matter how slight. Review your journal in light of the questions above, and share it with your partner or a trusted friend.

- Follow the beliefs–decisions–behaviors formula to reveal opportunities for growth: Beliefs lead to thoughts and decisions that prompt behaviors which provide opportunities for growth and change. (Use the example in the box below to help you.)

   Identify a belief about your child's potential, then list:

   - the thoughts that support that belief
   - the decisions that could flow from that belief
   - the behaviors that could follow
   - the opportunities for growth which would be created.

AN EXAMPLE OF BELIEFS TO BEHAVIORS

I identify a belief about my child's potential:

My child could someday show an animal at the county fair.

The thoughts that support that belief:

He likes animals, He is motivated by opportunities to care for animals; even though sometimes he gets overstimulated by the activity and movement of some animals.

The decisions that could flow from the belief:

We'll create opportunities for him to be around various animals to see which he likes and interacts with best.

The behaviors that could follow:

We take regular trips to our community farm and give him increasing time with the animals. We visit friends and neighbors with dogs and cats. We allow our son to choose a pet. We identify an aide that can support him when he volunteers at the community farm. We find our son find a friend the farm. We make a plan to phase out the aide over time.

The opportunities for growth:

Repeated exposure to various types of animals, opportunities to make choices, and repeated practice regulating his behavior in settings with multiple animals and other children increase his potential for caring for an animal and showing that animal at the county fair.

Listen to Your Child: Lean into Their Natural Curiosities to Build Agency and Skills, and Have Fun

YOU MADE A PERSON!

Clinicians told Kinesha and Steve that their son's IQ would never top 60. Julian's days consisted of various therapies punctuated by being carted along to his brother's baseball practices and games. Julian wanted nothing more than to be like those guys. In desperate moments he would repeat in measured tones, "I want to be like Collin, I want to play baseball." Hoping that "being like his brothers" might help Julian break through, Kinesha tried desperately to interest Julian in sports, signing him up for a parade of recreational and special teams, but the ball just could not hold his attention.

Julian spent most of his time in a world that his parents could not enter. They searched for signs that their son could maintain interest in anything. Kinesha worked tirelessly on simple directions like "Go to your bedroom and get your socks." On the way, Julian would inevitably get lost in an object that caught his eye—the socks long forgotten. Moments later that object too would be discarded as his interest meandered.

At about eight years old, almost by accident, Julian joined a couple of Lego pieces that made a simple mini Star Wars figure. Kinesha made a big deal about it: "Julian, you made a person!" Some days later, he pieced together a basic block structure. It wasn't much to look at, but Kinesha and Steve took notice. They started buying him basic Lego building sets. One by one, Julian mastered them, advancing to more complex models like working Ferris wheels and model sports cars. Over time, he was getting noticed for his Lego creations the same way his brothers had been for sports. As Julian's engineering skill outpaced the instruction manuals, he turned to creating elaborate structures purely from his imagination.

Kinesha indulged Julian's seemingly insatiable interest in Legos, while letting go of her expectation that he would follow in his brother's athletic footsteps.

Ironically, what began as "kid stuff" created the motivation for crucial grownup behaviors. Kinesha had Julian make lists of the prices for each Lego set or accessory that he wanted and required him to calculate the total. If the total was more than the amount he had to spend, she challenged Julian to take on the difficult task of "putting back" items he wanted until his calculations were back within his budget.

Kinesha and Steve recognized Julian's engineering skill as a significant accomplishment in its own right. But they also realized they could use his personal LOL, "Love of Legos," as a springboard to build critical life skills, including self-control, making choices, calculation, money management, motivation to work for money, and even understanding a timesheet.

Julian has moved far beyond Legos, but the skills they have instilled endure. Kinesha and Steve give credit to that little Star Wars person created one ordinary day.[1]

The Habit: Capable parents and caregivers listen to their child and lean in. They take notice of what their child says (and doesn't say). They follow behavioral clues that point to what makes their child feel happy and proud. They know the power of interests and passions in developing their child's mind and sense of self. They work to understand their child's curiosities and use this knowledge to build confidence, agency,

---

1   Julian is diagnosed with autism and ADHD.

and skills without being manipulative. They guide their child toward positive, fun, and productive expressions of their interests.

THE SCIENCE BEHIND THE HABIT

Regardless of challenge or diagnosis, kids are kids, and all kids are curious. But when it comes to childrearing the buck stops with us. We parents are charged with our child's nourishment, safety, and very existence. In the face of this weighty responsibility, it is understandable that we can get so caught up in the work of parenting that we miss out on the fun part. This is especially true if our child has medical complications that force all our attention to sustaining life.

But whether you are conscious of it or not, the progress that your child has already made is due largely to curiosity. Children are born with unbridled curiosity. In fact, if you are (or have ever been) the parent of a toddler, you know that a major part of your job description is to wipe down surfaces—toys, books, countertops, sometimes even siblings that are drool-soddened from the latest touch of their ever-exploring child. You simply can't keep a child from grabbing, touching, hitting, or gnawing on everything within reach. They explore the unfamiliar, until it is familiar. While touch is the typical modus operandi for early learning, if your child's mobility is severely limited they are still hungrily absorbing their world through whatever senses they can access, be it sight, hearing, or even smell.

Research has proven that dopamine, the brain's happiness chemical, is intricately linked to curiosity (Kidd and Hayden 2015). When kids explore and indulge their curiosity their brains reward their bodies with a flood of dopamine. This release of dopamine is at the root of how our kids' interests and passions generally make them feel calmer, happier, and more satisfied.

APPLYING THE HABIT

Parents, we all need to own it. We would be lying if we did not admit that we have things we would like our kids to do. The path we envision for our children is typically paved with the pursuits we ourselves feel comfortable with, enjoy, and love. Oftentimes they are tangled up with notions about the things that kids "should do." Things which were likely imprinted on us by our own families when we were young—just as those things were traced on our parents when they were young and their parents before them. "A chip off the old block," they say.

For our children with disabilities or who think differently, the universe of things we get caught up thinking they "should do" often extends to how they approach activities, how they play with toys, how they communicate their excitement, how they engage with others, and even what they get excited about. "The right way to play with a car is to push it on the ground, not hold it up in the air and watch the wheels spin," "Kids should get excited about playing outside, not memorizing facts about natural disasters," etc.

Letting go

Truly listening to your child means accepting and often necessitates letting go of what you want them to be interested in or what you think they should do. We all want the best for our children, regardless of their challenges, but all too often we parents use our age, wisdom, and our God-given status as protector-in-chief as pretext for channeling, cajoling, or even forcing our child into what *we think* they should be doing. Our rationale: we have survived this cruel world longer than our child, and as a result we believe we know better.

Without thinking, we use this stance as license to not listen to our child. I have counseled parents who have pushed their child into community college programs or into supported employment because that is what prevailing wisdom and the transition continuum says a young person in their position "should do." Listen to your child.

Hearing them does not mean you are giving up on goals and aspirations—you are just honoring their need for a breather.

Many of us have understandably been ensnared in the trap of pushing when we should have been listening. I am among these repentant souls. Here is how the ball bounced in our family—so to speak.

SHOOTING HOOPS

Instead of being hyperfocused on my son's limitations, I realized I could try to identify strengths, advantages, and potential motivators.

In my least proud parenting moments, I cringingly admit that I fell into the parenting pothole of thinking I alone knew what my child needed. I was so sure that I knew what would help him succeed and be accepted by peers, and allowed that to nudge out preferences he may have had.

Here is the thinking I used to justify the childhood equivalent of a veritable death march through all manner of recreational sports that my son may have preferred to avoid. "You are tall and lanky, people will expect you to play basketball, that will get you included and accepted." "You need muscle tone, body awareness, endurance, and coordination. What better way to turbo charge these skills than basketball practice?"

When I give myself grace, I remember that I am in kinship with the vast majority of parents whose fervor, no matter how misguided, came from a good place.

Had I truly listened and let go of what *I thought* would help him thrive and get him included, I might have done better by my son. It is true that Jack was a sports fan and that he needed physical skills and muscle development, but he was also into statistics and making lists, these were authentic passions. Perhaps if I truly tuned in and trusted my son, I would have suggested that he consider a role as ball boy, team manager, or statistician rather than a player on the team.

As I wised up, we began encouraging our son to volunteer at younger kids' sport camps which allowed him to be involved in a sport that he loved, to practice, get exercise, and work out without feeling pressure to perform. As a kicker, this emphasis on working with younger kids also helped Jack gain confidence and see himself as a leader.

When searching for activities, clubs, extracurriculars, or sports, leverage your child's strengths and natural proclivities. Avoid getting hyperfocused on their current limitations. If the entire activity is too much, identify and isolate the pieces of the activity that they can participate in and would enjoy.

For example, if it looks like your child enjoys a particular activity, but finds the pressure dysregulating and anxiety-provoking, consider having them participate as an observer or spectator, or have them serve in a volunteer capacity. This feeds their interest and promotes confidence and self-esteem, while turning down the temperature inherent in competition and performance expectations.

Instead of fixating on what they "should be" interested in, capable parents are always on the lookout for signs of their child's interests and curiosities. They pay attention to what their child seeks out when left to her own devices. They seek to:

- understand the function of interests or passions

- help their child find productive and appropriate ways to express those interests

- leverage their child's natural interests to nudge them toward expanded possibilities and build new skills.

Extraordinary interests

What should parents make of their child's unusual interests? The answer is a lot! The first order of business for parents raising a capable kid is understanding what their child is curious about, no matter how different those curiosities are from their own.

You may be thinking: Wait a minute! I am not that parent who is trying to live vicariously through my child. I am not hung up on my kid being into sports, playing Kick the Can, or collecting Pokémon cards. They don't have to be anything like me when I was a kid. I would be thrilled if my child was obsessed with Legos or balls, or bugs, or airplanes, or science, or dolls, or drawing, or climbing, or horses, or Dungeons & Dragons, or even spiders. But my child is consumed by unusual pursuits like touching fabric, stroking human hair or fur, watching wheels turn, feeling grains of sand slip through their fingers, squeezing a tattered piece of material, memorizing serial numbers on the back of small appliances, or reciting facts about hurricanes ad nauseum. If I leaned into my child's natural curiosities, I would find myself on my back all day staring at the rotating blades of ceiling fans.

Even the most empathic parent can be left scratching their head when their child's interests seem too intense, too unusual, or even strange. It may help to know that it is not only individuals who are neurodivergent or those with disabilities who have intense interests and fixations. Hyperfixation serves a useful biological function. It is common among young children because they are hard-wired to focus specifically on just a few things. How many parents remember reading their child the same *Thomas the Tank Engine* book until their eyes glazed over? Or who can recount tales of their four-year-old who would not take off his lion costume even to get into bed, far less to wash it?

Perceptions get complicated when intense passions persist beyond early childhood. Unfortunately, adults admire the kindergartener who proudly marches through the grocery aisles in his Transformers suit...*so cute and imaginative*, they say. But those same adults look with suspicion upon the 12-year-old who is doing the same thing.

Purposes of intense interests and fixations

Rather than getting caught up in how their child will be perceived, capable parents keep their eye on the prize. They remember that all behavior has a purpose. They seek to understand the function of their child's intense interests, fixations, or passions. Once understood, parents can support these interests, help their child channel them in safe, useful, and socially appropriate ways, and even capitalize on them to help their child gain new skills and competence.

Our child has an intense interest or fixation when they pay exclusive attention to or hyperfocus on one or a few things. Whatever it is, this thing is their "jam." It seems like they can't get enough of the particular object, topic, or behavior. Reluctance to set the object aside, change the subject, or transition to something different distinguishes intense interests from hobbies or casual diversions.

When we see our child engrossed in their intense interest for what seems like long stretches of time, we can get upset. I remember getting all wound up just thinking about all the "more important" things my son was not doing—like homework, communicating with us, enjoying the outdoors, or relating to other kids.

Listen to your child. What are they trying to tell you?

We have said that all behavior serves a purpose even if that purpose is not obvious to us at the moment. But what possible purpose could peeing in shampoo bottles, lining up shoes, or repeating the same rhyme over and over have?

Intense interests can calm our child, help them make sense of a complex world, decrease anxiety, and even build a positive self-concept. Your child's repetitive habit of fanning his fingers in front of his face may be relaxing them after an overwhelming day at school. Another child's insistence at examining and redrawing the same map over and over could be helping her make sense of what feels like threatening foreign territory. A child intently watching grains of sand slip through his fingers may be satisfying an innate curiosity around how light and color play on each grain of sand as it falls. A teen's stream of consciousness on tornadoes may be building his security and even self-esteem.[2]

---

2   For more on the benefits of special interests, see: www.spectrumnews.org/features/deep-dive/the-benefits-of-special-interests-in-autism

Determine how the interest is impacting your child and others

Is the intense interest causing pain to your child? Is it impeding your child's mastery of important skills? Is it getting in the way of friendships? Is it hurting or significantly disrupting others?

One wise dad, Hector, first was alarmed by his son Antonio's ear-twisting and face-squeezing. Based on his expression, he feared he was hurting himself. He was intent on holding his arms to his sides to prevent him from what he assumed was pain. Once Antonio could tell him that his ear-twisting and face-squeezing did not hurt, but quite the contrary it served to calm his overactive nervous system, Hector intuitively shifted his focus from extinguishing the behavior to encouraging his clever DIY self-soothing routine by teaching him to do it in the privacy of his own room or to excuse himself if he was in a public place. Hector recognized that his son knew exactly what he needed and encouraged him to take his calming routine to spaces that did not disrupt the classroom or the community.

If the intense interest is not dangerous to your child or others, worry less about eliminating it. In fact we rarely succeed in extinguishing a behavior, because if the underlying reason for the behavior persists, we can play whack-a-mole all day with specific behaviors that we don't like, but a new one will just pop up in its place. Instead focus on the positive function a behavior may be serving. Then you can determine how to support it in appropriate ways.

The upside of intense interests

Calming and sensory regulation are not the only potential upsides of intense interests. Your child's intense interest no matter how "niche" may actually be instrumental in building confidence and self-esteem. Competence is one of the two key aspects in self-esteem. Becoming an expert at something elevates feelings of competence and can lead to greater feelings of self-worth. Think about the satisfaction we get from our own special skills and talents. Whether you're a whiz at naming 90s hair bands, have a knack for guessing the specific spice in the foods you taste, or pride yourself on being able to dunk a basketball or do a backbend, our special traits make us feel good, sort of special...

at least in that narrow arena. The same is true for our kids whose interests diverge from the norm. Having a special skill (no matter how obscure) can be an important tally in the plus column for our kids who don't have a surplus of positive messages coming from the "typical centric" world around them.

Reciting lines from *Harry Potter* books and movies in character gave my son a sense of being recognized. This was particularly true when extended family members and friends joined him in the game of challenging each other on esoteric J.K. Rowling factoids. Jack's pride was unmistakable when other people turned to him as the expert judge for all things "HP."

Viva la interests!

Instead of trying to erase or squelch children's special interests, for years teachers have attempted to work them into the curriculum and the school day. Teachers find that when they lead with students' interests, they retain more and are willing to approach challenging tasks and learn things they would typically avoid. Similarly, psychologists are identifying ways to minimize the problematic side of having an intense interest without discouraging the overall interest itself. Like rewarding kids for pausing to ask about others' interests instead of talking exclusively about their own.

Capable parents are following suit by setting boundaries that allow their child to explore their interests in safe, productive, and appropriate ways. Regina's son's penchant for dissembling small appliances including the family's toaster, coffee maker, and microwave greatly disrupted mealtimes, until she bought a cartful of discarded appliances from a second-hand store for Simon to operate on, dissect, and explore.

Encourage your child to explore their interests in ways that build skills and social networks. A narrow interest in horses could lead to skills for navigating social situations and making friends if exercised in a horseback riding club or volunteer program for rehabilitating injured animals. When your child reaches an appropriate age, allow them to find their people in Facebook groups or appropriately monitored chat rooms. With the right internet controls you may encourage your child to create a website or a YouTube channel featuring their special interest.

Intense interests can be a vehicle to help a child understand their own behavior and relate to others. Once parents have a handle on their child's intense interest, they can get creative in identifying ways to use the interest to build skills and broaden their child's understanding of themselves. For example, if your child wants to talk about natural disasters to the exclusion of nearly everything else, you might use her deep knowledge of the Enhanced Fujita Scale (EF tornado classification system) to help her identify her mood and regulate her behavior. "I am feeling EF1 or EF2" may mean I'm a little off but I can use my strategies to stay calm, whereas "feeling EF4 or EF5" means I need to move to a safe spot because I am ready to blow.

In all these ways, an interest may help you meet your child where they are, make a connection, and build skills. I unapologetically took advantage of my own child's fascination with the open dishwasher door to build core strength and stamina.

It all started because of a slack sense of housekeeping and an open dishwasher door. Long before he was playing with toys appropriately, and while toddlers his age were exploring the world on two sturdy legs, Jack still had what I called "a baseboard" view of the world. Because he did not have the core strength to crawl on hands and knees, he would pull himself across the floor with his arms, his eyes at about "baseboard" height. He became obsessed with trying to lift his head to look into the dishwasher door and the yawning expanse inside. Fascinated, Jack began to pull on the door's edge that lay flat just a few inches above the floor—at about baseboard height. Taking notice, I had begun leaving the dishwasher door down on purpose—the shiny metal beckoning him to come inside and play. Before long Jack was dragging half and then nearly his whole body up and onto the dishwasher door. From that vantage point he could see into the milky white cave of dirty dishes. Jack saw it as fun, and I saw it as an unequivocal success. If curiosity could bait him to scale up and then pull his entire body weight up onto the door, what else could it get him to do? His curiosity and interest in what was at his eye level had coaxed more muscle and core stabilization work than months of visits to the physical therapist.

Beware of typecasting

Among the neurotypical and neurodivergent, we have all heard of preoccupations and passions that have led to acclaim and fortune. Satoshi Tajiri was nicknamed Mr. Bug as a child. His fascination with insects created the worldwide Pokémon craze.[3] Author, professor, and autism advocate Temple Grandin's intense interest in animals, particularly cows, led to an international revolution in how livestock are confined. Their intense interests may come to serve your child well. Your child's passions may support a career path, but they do not have to. Don't get caught in the trap of overemphasizing an interest to the point that you pigeonhole your child. There are many of us who "geek out" on putting together and sharing customized music playlists. That does not mean we all want to put our passion to work as wedding DJs. The same is true of our children. Don't conflate an intense interest with an ironclad career path.

A rose among thorns

But what to do when your child acts out an intense interest in inappropriate ways or in ways that may get him or her in trouble? Set clear boundaries and encourage your child to explore their passion in safe ways.

If you really pay attention to your child, you may identify parts of that passion or preoccupation that they *can* engage in socially acceptable and productive ways. A particularly curious 15-year-old with whom I worked, Jenny, loved the feel of fabrics against her skin, so much so that she would nuzzle up against any unsuspecting woman's fur coat collar or run her hand up and down a younger child's satin jacket. We helped Jenny create books that included samples of her

3   See https://the-art-of-autism.com/how-satoshi-tajiris-autism-helped-create-pokemon

favorite fabrics and encouraged her writing skills by challenging her to use descriptive words to communicate how each felt. Her interest in feeling fabrics persisted. In her late teens we found a job match for Jenny that accommodated her tactile interest in a way that was not only a value-add for the clothing store in which she worked, but also satisfying for her. In the role of "stocker" Jenny performed the fairly repetitive task of removing clothing items from their plastic packaging one by one, holding up their wire hanger with one hand, while lovingly running her other hand down the item smoothing out wrinkles as she hung it up. Unwrapping each garment satisfied her natural curiosity and sensory need to touch while presenting organized and appealing displays for the store's customers.

Threading the needle—always build on interests, never restrict them

Leveraging a passion or fixation can encourage learning and build vital skills. It is important to underscore that your child's interests should never be withheld as reward for them doing exclusively what you, the adult, wants. We want to support, build on, and use our child's interests to expand their world, not to "control" them.

Compassionate applied behavior analysis (ABA) advocates avoiding using an interest as a motivator or reinforcer for fear that it could taint a child's authentic interest. This is true if the interest is held hostage for "good behavior" or is denied for long periods of time. At the same time, I want to acknowledge that there are scores of families whose child has a highly narrowed interest. These are parents who are truly at a loss for finding something, anything, else that motivates their child. "Snakes are all he is interested in, I have nothing else to build upon," "All she attends to is videos on the iPad," etc. Capable parents are compassionate. They are able to thread the needle by listening to their child while also accessing the power of their child's passion to help them broaden their world and gain new skills that increase independence. Capable parents never use interests as a stick, but are masters at finding all kinds of ways to use them as a carrot. When we find ourselves in these situations, we reach our child by having them "slither" their socks into the hamper, count, add, and subtract the spots on snakes, mix the ingredients to roll out snake cookies, make a toothpaste snake on the brush, and the list goes on. Or in the iPad example we help them transition from seeing the iPad exclusively as an instrument for entertainment and calming their nervous system, to using it as a tool for finding information, using the light function to find something under the bed, and learning skills related to time, distance, and weather that affect them directly, like checking an app to figure out how to dress for the day.

Capable parents know when they need help. In most cases intense interests and repetitive behaviors are positive forces to be supported and channeled. They serve to calm, regulate nervous systems, and build self-esteem, but there are situations when interests cross over to obsessive patterns that are distressing to the individual. We know this to be true because individuals on the spectrum have voiced this phenomenon. Negative patterns include not being able to eat, losing sleep, and experiencing extreme anxiety while obsessively engaging in the interest or behavior. If you think your child may be at risk, a knowledgeable therapist or ABA professional can help.

Our kids' interests may be out of the norm but that does not mean they are abnormal. Here are three things to keep in mind:

- Interests wax and wane. When you are in the thick of it, it may seem like forever, but the fact is what your child is passionate about today will not always be their passion. Even intense interests change over time.

- You can "mine" pieces of an atypical interest to help your child build skills and social connections. You can help them maintain their interest in healthy, appropriate ways.

- You can be instrumental in helping your child find his people or places—other kids or contexts where the interest is shared and celebrated.

REFLECT...

Watch and listen to your child over the next week... Really watch and listen. Take note of what they do with free time. Ask yourself the following questions:

- What makes your child *happy* or *proud*? Look for not only verbal but behavioral cues.

- What can you learn from listening to your child?

- What activities, objects, and/or sensory activities is your child drawn to?

- How can you help them find their voice through interests?

- How could you lean in to interests to build skills?

- Break down extracurricular activities or sports into their component parts or steps to identify the parts that your child enjoys. Are there specific pieces of an extracurricular activity in which your child is strong or finds motivating? Encourage ways to participate that feature your child's preferred parts.

- How and where can you look for unexpected opportunities for your child to fulfill an interest or passion?

- Where can you find opportunities for your child to lead or share expertise?

TRY IT ON...

- Lean in to your child's interest or passion. Pay attention and watch your child as they engage in their interest or passion. Determine the function of the interest or passion. Is it:

- calming?

- nervous system regulating?

- competence or confidence building?

Determine the trade-offs of the interest or passion. Is it:

- hurting your child?

- hurting or disrupting others?

- getting in the way of learning, socializing, or other priorities?

Use this information to determine how you want to lean in to the interest or passion. You can choose to:

- encourage the interest for its positive effects

- leverage the interest to broaden your child's world, take on new challenges, create opportunities, and/or build additional life skills and competencies

- work with your child to get them to express their interest in positive ways.

• Identify an activity, object, or sensory activity to which your child is naturally drawn. Lean in to this natural curiosity to entice her to take on a new challenge, expand the interest, or learn a new skill.

Set a Vision of Capable with
Your Child and Adjust It over Time

MORE THAN ONE WAY...

Long before favorite teachers and case managers had uttered the word, Rene had been researching this thing called "transition," which signaled that magical age where his son Mateo's school day would morph from focusing on academics to getting him ready for adult life. Besides Mateo, Rene had two grown children with jobs. He never lost an opportunity to "talk up" Maria who did internet marketing and Jorge who was a freelance code writer.

His youngest son Mateo loved people and enjoyed nothing more than clowning around to get laughs. The kid had customer service written all over him, Rene thought. A lower IQ would not keep Mateo from working—Rene was sure of it. He believed that Mateo would be employed, like his brother and sister before him.

Rene treated Mateo in ways that were consistent with that vision. He started early offering Mateo money for small chores, teaching him the value of a dollar. He often had Mateo ride along with him on visits to his landscaping clients. Mateo grew up seeing how his dad offered little extras to keep satisfied customers coming back.

The day Mateo passed out in the high school cafeteria, doctors offered a second diagnosis, Type 1 diabetes—Rene felt the vision for Mateo dissolving. It was like a black cloud had come home to roost. Dealing with this serious condition was a full-time job, so much so that

Rene's wife had taken classes to become a caregiver just to manage the medical intricacies of their son's delicate blood-sugar dance. They both knew ignoring a single reading could be life-threatening.

One day as he was wrapping up a fountain installation job at the community senior center, Rene let his imagination wander. And as he did, he wondered if his own hyperfocus on "work" had him thinking too narrowly. Maybe there was another path for his youngest son. Could Mateo put his big personality to use in someplace like this? Maybe not as an employee...not yet...but as a volunteer...an apprentice? Rene visibly squinted as he attempted to bring this new idea into focus, while simultaneously ringing Mateo's transition coordinator.

Before long Mateo was playing games with the senior center residents, making them laugh at his sometimes clever, sometimes corny jokes. Over time he memorized each of the residents' names along with their favorite games: Gus liked Uno, Marion loved Sorry... This was a part-time assignment that Mateo could manage while he and his mom "managed" his diabetes through a new phone app.

Rene wells up with pride whenever the residents' sons, daughters, and sometimes even grandchildren stop him in the hallway to rave about how their loved one watches the clock until Mateo arrives in the Rec room for game time.

Today friends can hear Rene boasting about all three of his kids, Maria the Marketing Manager, Jorge the Computer Programmer, and Mateo, the Activities Assistant Coordinator at the Senior Community Center.[1]

The Habit: Capable parents set down a vision of what capable looks like *with* their child. The vision is firmly rooted in "the present" but is bold enough to imagine "the possible." The vision describes facets of meaningful life given your child's interests, preferences, skills, and passions. It is owned by your child but is informed by you as the person who knows your child best. Once crafted it serves as the litmus test for accommodations, supports, modifications, and services

---

1   Mateo is diagnosed with Williams syndrome/Type 1 diabetes.

that come your child's way and it defines the opportunities parents seek to encourage. They revise and adjust the vision with their child over time.

THE SCIENCE BEHIND THE HABIT

Visioning allows us to assign relative value to desired states, which allows us to narrow down and focus on what we truly value and to set priorities. The science behind visioning has been popularized by vision boards. Imagining a positive future is one way to increase positive emotions and optimism. And positive emotions often help us take advantage of opportunities and increase our chances for success.

As difficult as it is to hold on to competing ideas of what is true now (warts and all) and what is possible, it turns out that, for our brains, toggling between current and desired future states is critical for reaching goals. The comparison between what *is now* and what the future *could be* sets up an unambiguous contrast that provides direction, clarity, and motivation.

APPLYING THE HABIT

Visions of capable are not fantastical images one might imagine being conjured by a psychic gazing into a crystal ball. Our "vision of capable" is something that is both tangible and actionable. We are speaking specifically about a shared belief about your child's future which is informed and shaped by their interests, motivations, and passions, as well as by your hopes for them.

A vision of capable does not mean "curing" your child. Although, as we have said, there is not a parent alive who would not wish an easier time for their child, "curing" feeds unrealistic, unhelpful, and largely deficient thinking about our child. Curing misses the point and fuels the narrative that difference is something that needs to be eradicated. We only have to look to such extraordinary humans as

Dan Aykroyd, Simone Biles, Albert Einstein, Bill Gates, Tim Burton, Temple Grandin, Elon Musk, and Michael Phelps, all labeled as neurodivergent, to know that different thinking does not equal deficient thinking.

Parents who are raising their kids to be capable regardless of their challenges are not parents in denial. They realize their child's current limitations. But because they believe that effort creates potential within their child (see Habit #1), and because they are in tune with their child's natural curiosities, interests, and motivations (see Habit #2), they have the raw material to imagine what is possible for their child. They use this understanding to shape short- and long-term visions of capable. Finally, they adjust these visions as their child's interests, passions, skill levels, and opportunities evolve over time.

The many faces of capable

As stated in the Introduction, the dictionary defines *capable* as an adjective meaning "having power and ability." I define it as an individual living a meaningful life (as defined by them and the people who love them) with maximum agency that they can access. That is a mouthful, but when we get right down to it, isn't that what we all want for our kids, neurodivergent or otherwise—to live a life of meaning that they choose?

Because neurodiversity captures a broad swath of the population—as we have said an estimated 1 in 5 school-age children identify as neurodivergent or having a disability—"capable" takes on a multitude of faces. For one child, "living a meaningful life with maximum agency" looks like using their assistive communication device to actively participate in class discussions. For another, it looks like mastering the time-management, impulse-regulation, and planning skills necessary to access college. For a third, it is learning the "rules" of social communication involved in making friends and sustaining them over time. Perhaps for another individual, "capable" is recognizing the signals necessary to manage their own toileting so that they are able to take part in after-school clubs and social activities. Finally capable could be successfully joining the girl scouts, a gaming club that meets online, or maintaining a chat room for Anime enthusiasts. The list is endless. Suffice it to say, there are as many faces of "capable" as there are individual children and families.

Whose vision is it anyway?

My research bears out the fact that those raising strong, capable, curious humans do hold a tangible (even if changing) vision of what success looks like for their child. But whose vision is it anyway? Young children may not directly articulate the vision but they are shaping it when they "show" parents their interests, curiosities, and proclivities. Parents rely on observation to set this vision. As their child matures they increasingly build this vision with their child. Capable parents ensure that their child's voice is predominant.

As your child's role in vision-setting expands, you send the message loud and clear that his or her voice matters, that they are valued, and that they are capable. Together parents and child revise the vision over time as context, needs, and interests change.

Disability self-advocates have championed the mantra "nothing for me without me" and for good reason. For the majority of documented history people with disabilities have been treated as "less than"—at best "hapless angels" to be cared for and pitied, at worst subhuman burdens. Advocates have done the heavy lifting to put disability inclusion on the map. They have caused us "normees" to finally sit up, take notice of and respect all the amazing minds, bodies, and hearts that come in diverse packages and express their ideas in unique ways.

Ensuring that our child's voice is at the center of the capable vision is critical, but respecting our child's agency does not mean parents are relegated to the role of marginalized bystander. Maximizing our child's voice does not mean we parents recede into the woodwork. It is neither practical nor advisable for parents to abdicate their responsibility for helping chart their child's course. Some parents I have worked with initially swore that they did not hold a vision for their child's future, but rather simply followed their child's lead. At first blush that sounds admirable and in lock step with the "nothing for me without me" philosophy. As we dug deeper together, those parents acknowledged that they did in fact have very real ideas of what they wanted for their child and that these ideas did inform their thoughts, decisions, and actions.

Notwithstanding the critical role of the child in crafting their own destiny, parents figure centrally in the process for two reasons. First, all children (including neurotypicals) are disadvantaged due to lack of experience and maturity. If I were to surrender to my daughter's "vision of capable" when she was 14, it would have been to be able to watch YouTube videos and doom scroll social media all night, while fitting in school work into the crevices in between. Second, depending on their developmental age, cognitive-processing level, and communication skills, children vary in their reliability and accuracy when it comes to getting across their preferences.

There is a healthy interplay between children's interests and parents' knowledge of their child when vision-setting. This quick example illustrates it. Davidson's 13-year-old son Kareem wanted nothing to do with a bike. To him bikes were scary, they rocked his touchy vestibular system, challenged his balance, and were just "all round" too chaotic and risky. He preferred riding in the front seat of his dad's gleaming sedan and his sister's junker, or if neither of those was available, he would just as soon walk. But his dad knew something about Kareem that Kareem had yet to fully discover about himself. Kareem liked getting out of the house and experiencing new things. One of his favorites was eating at restaurants. Because of cognitive impairment, driving a car of his own someday was not an option for Kareem. Davidson also recognized that he would not be around forever to drive his son to all his favorite spots.

So while Davidson knew that 13-year-old Kareem would not choose it, he began to imagine that his son would someday independently use a bicycle to navigate their close-knit community. He knew that bike lanes and designated bike trials could get his son to many of the restaurants, fast-food joints, and stores he loved. His dad held on to the vision and began to create opportunities for Kareem to get more comfortable with two-wheeled transportation. He first used a tandem bike with him navigating and Kareem in the back, then a large three-wheel bike, and a bike without pedals. With these supports and the reality check of his dad letting Kareem know that he was not available to "chauffeur" most nights, Kareem gradually developed the motivation and balance to ride a bicycle independently. In this way he helped Kareem secure a future where he would be able to engage in many of his favorite pastimes without someone else in the driver's seat. Today Kareem is proud of his independence (although he still lets his dad drive occasionally) and is glad that his dad weighed in and encouraged this new path to independence he could not imagine as a young teen. When interviewed, grownup Kareem admitted that if his dad left it all up to him "he would probably still be sitting at home bored."

A vision of capable and the IEP

The Individual Educational Plan (IEP) can be a helpful tool in the process of raising a capable kid. However, when I talk about setting a vision of capable, I am not talking about specific IEP goals written in behavioral terms. Statements like 'Jaden will approach new people she wants to engage with an outstretched hand with 80% accuracy over ten consecutive opportunities' or 'Tonia will independently submit required math assignments on or before the assigned due date 80% of the time over the eight-week marking period' are not visions of capable.

To be sure, your child's IEP should be based on data describing your child's interests, strengths, and challenges. These precision goals and objectives are important. They communicate priorities, keep the eyes of kids, teachers, and therapists on the prize, and break down complex behaviors into manageable bites. They are critical, but IEP goals without a vision can become myopic or out of step with the bigger picture for your child's future if they are not monitored carefully.

The vision of capable is not just one giant IEP goal, nor is it a mandated part of the IEP process. However, a clear vision of capable should inform the IEP. Parents, as their child's first teacher and the ones who likely know their child best, should come to the IEP process with their vision of capable in mind and should use it to inform the course of the IEP.

What a sound vision does

You may think, what difference does a vision make, it is only words. True, your vision of capable is only as good as how you use it to shape opportunities for your child. You may say "I know what I want for my child." That is great, most of us do—now get good at articulating it.

Think of the vision of capable as a tool for activating our intentions. When we get tired, overwhelmed, or scared, waters in which we parents of children with disabilities often tread, we are likely to abandon our well-crafted intentions and let our brain stems do our thinking for us. Physicist and *Seat of the Soul* author Gary Zukav says that intention is the most powerful force we possess (Zukav 1999). Our vision of capable, set with our child, is a constant reminder of our intention and helps us act in ways that are *intentional* when responding to our child and making decisions that affect them. Even though we (with our child) will likely revise our vision many times over the course of their childhood, we are better off than if we had no vision at all, nothing to frame our intentions.

The vision will make all the difference for your child, but only if you *use* it. Once set, capable parents use this vision as their litmus test or "North Star" in carrying out the laundry list of decisions they are charged with making with and for their child every day.

Setting a vision of capable

There are four steps in crafting a vision of capable.

1. *Understand "the present."* Come to terms with the present or "what is" for your child. In order to do this it is important to understand your child's current reality. Only when you clearly see where your child "is" can you imagine where they may go. This involves looking at your child's current state "warts and all" with dispassionate clarity.

- Answer this question: Today, what are my child's strengths, weaknesses, exceptionalities, and blindspots?

2. *Identify sparks of potential.* Sparks of potential are positive movement or successes (no matter how small) that you have witnessed. Take note of what has worked (and what has not) for your child in the past. Use what you have observed and know about your child's personality traits, motivations, interests, and natural curiosities.

   - Answer these questions: What progress has my child made to date and what has caused it? What unexpected sparks of potential have I seen? Are there special opportunities or circumstances I need to consider?

3. *Imagine "the possible."* Given your responses to the questions in 1 and 2, imagine and visualize what your child may do, master, achieve, or become in the timeframe under consideration.

4. *Set a vision.* Write your vision of capable in a couple of sentences. Adjust it over time with your child's growing voice, context, and experience.

Here is how the four steps crystalized in an early vision of capable with my seven-year-old:

1. *Understand "the present."* My child is not holding a pencil, crayon, or pen with a tripod grasp, a skill his siblings had mastered seemingly effortlessly by age three. Therapists' efforts with specialized hand grips and our tries at using DIY pencil grips made from ponytail elastics are not working. The multitude of tiny muscles and tendons in the center of his hand that contract in concert to hold a pencil are slack. When he holds a pencil or crayon without a grip it dips forward. His printing is laborious and difficult to read. He tires easily and complains when he has to "write" for school work. He loves technology, and while he is not proficient at the keyboard, he is pecking at the keys.

2. *Identify sparks of potential.* Jack loves reading and being read to. When left to his own devices, he would prefer turning pages in a book to almost anything. He likes the idea of creating his own stories, even if not physically writing them. He wants to be like other kids in his second-grade class. Because all the second-grade boys are drawing superheroes, I was surprised to see him drawing in his notebook as well.

3. *Imagine "the possible."* I imagine him participating with his class in activities that require printing and writing. I imagine him proudly sharing superhero pictures he creates. I envision him living on his own someday and needing to leave notes for a roommate to pick up milk or toilet paper at the store. I imagine him doodling and jotting notes for stories he has.

4. *Set a vision.* My son will learn to write with his hand. He will be able to sign documents that require a signature, and he will have the option to decide whether he wants to capture his ideas on paper or digitally.

In order to create a working vision, it is necessary to hold two competing ideas in our heads at the same time: current circumstances or "what is" which can be painful to stare down in the moment, and the promise of "what is possible." When we hold these two sacred, we remain grounded in reality, while imagining and focusing on potential. What might my child do tomorrow, next time, next week, next year, in adulthood?

The timeframe

You can use these four steps to create a vision for any timeframe that is reasonable to expect change. If your child is in elementary school, you might create a vision of capable for the next transition point, say middle school. If they are in middle school, you might revise that vision for high school, and from high school to adulthood. The timeframe matters less than that the vision is solidly rooted in the present and uses your child's voice and what you know about them to imagine what is possible. Below is a sequence of visions that I held for my child.

Vision of capable with my child (revised over time):

- Ages 1–4: Jack will share the same experiences as his twin sister.

- Ages 5–7: Jack will walk with arms lowered from full to partial guard and then to his sides.

- Ages 8–11: Jack will have the option to express his ideas on the computer or by writing with his hand.

- Ages 12–14: Jack will maintain his school work while reducing special education supports and will exit special education.

- Ages 15–18: Jack will go to college.

- Long term: Jack will live independently.

There are as many uniquely beautiful visions of capable as there are children and families on this earth. Because each one is rooted in the child's current reality and takes into account the child's interests, passions, skills, and motivations, they are tethered to reality while at the same time acknowledging that effort and opportunity are the jet fuel of potential to future successes.

Imagine the possible...while being honest about the present.

The vision involves holding sacred two competing ideas simultaneously: *imagining the possible while being honest about the present*. The following table shows additional examples of holding "the present" and "the possible" in your head at the same time.

What is now...	What could be...
My teenage daughter loves toddlers and preschoolers so much. She reaches for them and hugs them, which makes parents fearful and annoyed.	Someday...she will play games and organize snack time with kids while working at the local daycare center with the support of a job coach.
My eight-year-old loves outings but is excluded from activities because she does not recognize and communicate her need to use the bathroom.	Someday...she will be included in field trips because she will reliably use her communication device to signal her personal care needs.
My son turns away every time the ball is tossed in his direction—but he likes to feel and hold the ball.	Someday...he will play basketball.
My daughter gets overstimulated when she is around children her age, which leads to screaming and holding her hands over her ears, but she loves caring for animals.	Someday...she will care for her own animal and show it at the county fair.
My son is creative and loves imaginative play, but other kids avoid playing with him because he can't get his thoughts out quickly and often repeats what others have just said, which kids make fun of.	Someday...he will be a regular member of an online Dungeons & Dragons group.

The ideal vision should be a few sentences. Think of it as an "elevator speech." It is a memorable statement that you can communicate in the time it takes to get from one floor to the next.

Okay, you have crafted a vision of capable that is squarely grounded in the present. It considers your child's unique motivations, personality traits, interests, and passions in identifying what is possible. Now the question remains: How do we get from here to there? There are two tips for actually getting to the vision. First, make the vision come alive by using it for decision-making. Second, focus on doable baby steps toward the vision.

A living vision

The vision once crafted becomes a living statement. It is not just a bunch of happy-sounding words strung together. It is active. It is the reality-based, forward-looking expression of a meaningful life for your child. It provides the guard rails or boundaries as you go through daily life with your child. It helps you decide among existing opportunities and seek out new ones for and with your child. You use it as the "litmus test" or decision-making guide for the supports, services, accommodations, and modifications that are offered to your child and for those that you request from doctors, case managers, the school system, ABA providers, and doctors.

If the vision is that your child will learn alongside peers in classrooms of 25 students, you may seek out short-duration friends groups and kids yoga classes that help your child gradually adjust to the sound and activity levels that they will encounter in the classroom. At the same time you may say no to "pull-out" reading fluency practice in the resource classroom because it does not align with your vision of your child learning with peers. You may choose instead to get your child a reading tutor outside of school hours to maximize in-class time with peers.

If the vision is that your child will be an active member of the community, you may point teachers toward expanded opportunities to practice self-care skills during the day so that he can participate in community outings where independent toileting is necessary. This vision can direct the occupational therapist to focus on building interoception skills so that your child builds the body awareness necessary for them independently to signal that they have to use the bathroom. This vision may increase your resolve not to resort to pull-ups, but to work on toileting at home.

It may feel like not even a bell-bottomed Evel Knievel, circa 1973, would attempt to jump the chasm between where your child "is now" and "what is possible." So then how is it that we are to maintain unbounded hope day after day, despite the harsh glare of reality?

It is the promise of what might come next that becomes the precious renewable fuel for expectations. It is important to intentionally train yourself to acknowledge your child's limitations while refusing to get mired down in the heaviness of "what is." I focused on what I came to call "the power of next."

When we first saw the light in Jack's eyes at the dining room table, we thought what is the next object of interest that those eyes will capture? When he lifted his head ever so slightly, we dangled the toy a little higher, imagining how he might lift an inch or two more. When he leaned against the train table to substitute for core strength, we pulled the table away slightly so that he had to stabilize and reach further to run the engine along the tracks. When he grasped a pencil whole-fisted, we made a pencil grip out of two elastic hair ties that forced him to hold the pencil back between his thumb and forefinger. Modest gains for sure, but each one was inching Jack closer to the vision.

Planting my feet on the path and training my gaze on the next anthill rather than the mountains that loomed in the distance was how I nourished hope. Focusing on the mountain would be enough to break anyone. We came to call this "Jack's next 15 yards," borrowing from another very real chasm I personally had to bridge.

The next 15 yards

My husband and I first learned to ski in the Colorado Rockies. Anyone who has skied Colorado knows these are not bunny hills. The way down starts at 12,000 feet. To us, not particularly athletic 30-somethings clinching our knees, making wide turns, our skis locked in classic pizza formation, the base looked impossibly distant. It was a place we would never reach. The day we shared a single lesson, as that was what we could afford, I listened intently, hanging on to the ski instructor's every word as if for dear life. We stood poised over the vertical expanse that lay between our teetering skis and the horizontal security of the base below. I repeated his words all the way down the mountain. "Don't look at the base, keep your eyes fixed 15 yards ahead, and when you reach that point, fix on the next 15 yards." And so we moved from the impossibility of a 12,000-foot summit to the gloriously flat terra firma below. Allowing ourselves to visualize only a stingy 15 yards at a time. That is how I think it is with hope for our kids.

On the edge of each small success lies the come-hither promise of the next, similar to Vygotsky's "zone of proximal development."[2] We can grasp that which is close to where we are currently. Try for something too distant, too ambitious, and we fail discouraged. But identify that which is directly above or adjacent to where we are, and we will seek it and achieve.

Don't become discouraged because the vision feels distant, focus your attention on the next doable step—those precious next 15 yards. For us, that was jerryrigging a pencil grip that would comfortably seat the pencil at an angle in Jack's hand and doing hand grip exercises. For Angela's daughter Aiden, the next 15 yards toward her vision of enjoying meals together in restaurants was wearing noise-canceling headphones for short periods of time in the high school cafeteria. For Karissa's son Calvin, the next 15 yards toward what seemed like a distant vision of independent hygiene was helping him satisfy his tactile needs by playing with a bit of shaving cream on a whiteboard after using the toilet instead of smearing feces. Keeping the vision of capable in mind, what is your child's next 15 yards?

REFLECT...

* What specific ideas of competence do you hold for your child?

* Where would you like them to be in two years, five years, as an adult?

2　Vygotsky, L.S. (1978). For an explanation of the zone of proximal development, see www.simplypsychology.org/zone-of-proximal-development.html

- What have you observed in your child that indicates his preferences, interests, and passions? (See Habit #2.)

- What sparks of potential have you observed in your child?

TRY IT ON...

- Follow the four steps set out above to craft a vision of capable with your child:

  a. Understand "the present."

  b. Identify sparks of potential.

  c. Imagine "the possible."

  d. Set a vision.

- Given the vision, identify the "next 15 yards" for your child. Considering "what is" for your child currently, identify the next doable step toward the vision. Identify opportunities for them to practice the next step and commit to practice them.

Put the Diagnosis in Its Place, Your Child Is a Kid First

WHY NOT?

Samantha smiles, recalling feeling like a frazzled assembly line worker. She fell behind again, peeling and separating mandarin orange sections, so quick was 22-month-old Macy at scooping them up, savoring even the tiny juice droplets that escaped down her chin. Then she remembers the morning not long after when Macy could no longer scoop, her hands rhythmically wringing. The abrupt loss of the use of her hands was yet another indicator that all was not well.

This was the alarming pattern that led up to her diagnosis—Macy met milestones slowly and seemed to lose skills that she had once mastered. Samantha reflects that Macy had rolled and then stopped rolling. She had reached for toys and then stopped reaching.

Samantha nursed nagging suspicions, and did her share of googling symptoms: "low muscle tone, sleepy, poor feeder," etc. At ten months, when Macy was not sitting up, doctors had chalked it up to her being a "lazy baby." Not satisfied, Samantha and her husband began searching for answers to their daughter's puzzling behavior. This led to seemingly endless rounds of blood work, MRIs, and painful nerve-conduction assessments. Finally came the genetic testing.

Samantha describes hearing her daughter's diagnosis over the phone like the cannon shot that catapults her into a black hole. A natural fighter, she found herself at a total loss. Her first instinct was denial. "Not Macy, she will be the exception to the rule." Her second was anger: "Why my daughter? Why me?"

Today, nearly six years later, when it comes to Macy, Samantha no longer asks "Why?" but "Why not?" Wherever the diagnosis proclaims limitations, Samantha looks for possibilities. When the diagnosis says "children with Macy's condition can't communicate," Samantha furrows her brow and says, "Why not?" Samantha explains it this way: "The diagnosis is all hung up on the 'verbal' part. With technology Macy can communicate! It is *her* voice, *her* humor, *her* sassiness, *her* heart coming through her eye-gaze activated assistive communication device."

Yes, Macy has a syndrome, but more importantly, she is a little human who likes to experiment with makeup and play with dolls just like other seven-year-olds. And to that Samantha says, "Why not?"[1]

The Habit: Parents who raise their child to be capable put their child's diagnosis in its place. They know that their child is a complex individual who has much more in common with other kids than a laundry list of symptoms. Capable parents see their child's diagnosis or label for what it really is—information to be used, not the determiner of who their child is or who they will become.

Even disability self-advocates who lead with their label acknowledge that a person is infinitely more complex than their diagnosis. There are autistic people who train in mixed martial arts, and those who prefer not to be touched; there are people with ADHD who thrive in quiet, and those who need to work with a buzz of activity around them; there are introverts with intellectual disabilities who recharge by being alone, and extroverts who get energy from being in the midst of humanity; there are those with cerebral palsy who express their creativity through dance (despite their wheelchairs), and others who paint, draw, or write. If a person "is their diagnosis" we would not see the literally endless array of individual differences between people bearing identical diagnostic labels.

Capable parents use the diagnosis for the explanations, services,

---

1   Macy has Rhett syndrome.

and support it can afford their child. Most of all, they are careful not to get caught up in the trap of "expecting to see" the characteristics described in their child's diagnosis.

THE SCIENCE BEHIND THE HABIT

The human brain wants to sort and categorize. It wants to file information into tidy mental drawers so it can make sense of what it perceives. That is in part why diagnoses, no matter how dire, often have a strangely comforting quality to them. They apply a thick salve of reason and explanation to our child's confounding behavior or physiological responses. "Oh that explains why he doesn't turn toward me when I call his name," "Now I understand why she never developed a strong suck when I tried so hard to nurse," "When I assumed he was just 'zoning out,' those were, in fact, small seizures," or "Oh, that is why she grimaces with her hands over her ears until everyone in the car has their seatbelt fastened and the beeping stops."

The fact that our brains crave order and explanation makes labeling compelling—useful knowledge we seek out and latch on to. This piece of human evolution gives our brains solace in the face of diagnosis.

There is a second part to how our brain reacts to labeling, and it is equally important because it determines how we process diagnostic information and how labels affect us. The confirmation bias principle has proven time and time again that *what* we think about a person's intellect, social desirability, and health impacts how we treat them (Childcare Education Institute 2021; Nickerson 1998). Or, in addition, another scientific principle called the primacy effect makes our brains naturally glom on to the first bits of evidence we receive in a confounding situation.[2] This makes parents susceptible to believing in all the indications offered in our child's initial diagnosis—even ones that their child doesn't exhibit.

....

2   For some examples, see https://practicalpie.com/primacy-effect-examples

When we begin "to expect" to see each characteristic of our child's diagnosis, something happens within us. We make subtle and not so subtle changes in how we *behave* toward our child. In practice I have seen how these behavioral shifts on our part can actually lead to our child manifesting characteristics of the diagnosis that we expect.

Scientists at Stanford University in California are exploring exactly how powerful a person's beliefs are. They have evidence that merely receiving information about a genetic condition can affect not only a person's beliefs, but even their physiology, in ways that may increase their risk for the condition being tested. Researchers found that being told you're more likely to develop a condition can, in some cases, result in real physiological changes, including elevated heart rates and reduced activity levels, that trump the actual risks for the condition, suggesting that our mindset may be more important than even our biology when it comes to our health (Turnwald *et al.* 2019).

So if a person's behavior and physiology can be impacted by what they *believe* about their condition, it naturally follows that the messages that parents send their child about their diagnosis are critical. We'll explore these messages more in Habit #6, but the important thing to remember is that the mindset you adopt when your child receives their diagnosis is not irrelevant. It can alter how you feel about your child, what you do with them, and how you respond to them.

APPLYING THE HABIT

What the diagnosis is and is not

Knowing how our brains react to diagnoses and labels makes it vitally important that parents are intentional about putting the diagnosis in its place. Although it is natural to respond initially with a barrage of strong emotions, capable parents come to a place where they make peace with the diagnosis without allowing it to define their child. Having first put it in its place, they are then able to put the diagnosis to use to get their child the support and services they need to improve his or her daily life.

Navigating the River "De-nial"

No matter how awe-inspiring the child before you, any diagnosis is a signal that our beautiful creation just does not "measure up" to the standards of this world—no matter how unfair, misleading, or inaccurate. It is bound to trigger some level of grief. No two people grieve the same way, and not all parents go through the same stages. However, the strong emotions that parents may go through after a diagnosis map onto the classic stages of grief: denial, anger, bargaining, depression, and acceptance. Grief happens. Throughout our lives loss of a relationship, marriage, job, home, loved one, or even a pet can trigger it. While each of these is devastating, triggering ripples of loss that last well beyond the event, *the events* that produced the grief are one-time occurrences—a death, a job loss, divorce. However, parents of kids with disabilities often experience what is called cyclical grieving (Blaska 1998). Cyclical grieving is when you feel earlier stages of the grieving process, that you may have thought you had gotten over again and again. We are triggered back to anger or depression each time our child's friends or siblings master developmental milestones before them or have experiences that we think are inaccessible to our child. "My child will never be on a team," "My child will never go to prom," "My child will never drive," or "My child will never have a true friend to clown around with." These recurring emotions are normal, we should not be ashamed of them. We should talk about them with others and use these conversations to confirm the fact that we are not alone.

DIARY OF A RECOVERING PARENT

I share part of my diagnosis story because it offers a window on some of the stages of grief. See if you can pick them out. Do any ring true to your child's diagnosis story?

Descending the rabbit hole

After an indeterminate number of minutes, which my mind morphed into hours, we were ushered back into Dr. Stuart's office. "Mrs. Winking," he said unceremoniously, "because of Jack's unusually rapid growth and persistent developmental delays, I suspect that he has a syndrome." His tone was roughly that of a grocery store clerk helping me locate the olives on aisle 11. Not the tenor you would expect to accompany the bottom dropping out of your world. There, he had said it, the dirty S-word. I scanned my brain for a list of familiar syndromes... Down syndrome..., Rhett syndrome..., Williams syndrome, Stockholm syndrome... No wait, that was something else altogether. I shook off the bizarro diversion.

I began conjuring images of the developmental delays, intellectual impairments, and physical ailments that were associated with each condition.

As if in a vortex, all of the oxygen was being sucked out of the room. I wanted to take my babies and get out, not hear what was coming out of this guy's mouth. It was all so incongruent with the day I had imagined for us when my feet hit the floor that morning. If I could just rewind roughly the last 30 seconds. God, let me rewind.

Jack had seen scads of doctors, for Chrissake, he was a preemie. If there was a syndrome to be found, any one of the army of esteemed medical personnel who attended to him would have caught it, wouldn't they?

I wanted to run, but I was rooted to the Berber carpet. Stuart was still talking. "Focus, Deb, he is saying something about foreheads?" It took all my energy to force myself out of my thoughts and back into the cold reality of the room, back into the interrogation. This guy was actually rattling off a textbook list of symptoms.

"Jack has a broad forehead," he said. I had never liked to show my own. My mother once told me I had a forehead "that you could paint a sign on." That was precisely why since second grade I had sported a thick set of bangs, which could double as a barometer for how reliably they spiraled up like uneven bed springs with a rise in humidity. I rarely unveiled my forehead to the public, but this was go time. To deflect the arrows now directed toward Jack, I lifted my auburn fringe. "See, I have a big forehead too," I announced matter-of-factly, as if this revelation would put an end to this insanity. Ha! The brilliant doctor was detecting simple heredity, not a syndrome.

He barely acknowledged my defensive move and continued down his list. "Jack has a long face," he said. Again, I chimed in, "So do I." He has a pointy chin. He has large, wide-set eyes. Now his observations were coming at me in rapid-fire succession. Reeling from the craziness of it all, I checked out again for a few seconds. My thoughts drifted to the sanguine, big-foreheaded porcelain figurines of my youth, circa 1976. Relying on humor to defuse anger was a familiar tactic of mine. "Doctor, are you saying my son has 'Precious Moments' syndrome?" Dr. Stuart continued, not even cracking a smile.

His dad and I had dismissed Jack's developmental delays as nothing more than a preemie variation of typical. No one had connected the dots to a diagnosis. The doctor was still talking, but now I needed answers. My mind breezed over the physical characteristics he described. A pointy chin, wide-set eyes, and high forehead I could handle. I was interested in characteristics that significantly altered or shortened lives. I desperately needed to know whether this fast-growing, big-foreheaded, pointy-chinned syndrome was life-threatening? I flooded Stuart with questions. "Yes, doctor, but is it degenerative? Is it hereditary? Does it cause learning problems?"

He was still talking, but it did not matter; by now Dr. Stuart's voice had taken on the rhythmic nasal quality of the teacher in every Charlie Brown Special: "Wha wha wha wha, wha." The guy had lost me at "I don't fully know all the attributes of the syndrome" and now he was wasting precious time. By now I had dismissed polite conventions like "thank you" and "goodbye" as counterproductive. I had already pointed the stroller in the direction of the door and was careening down the hall into a conveniently positioned elevator, leaving skid marks on Dr. Stuart's tasteful, steel blue Berber.

What would this new word mean for Jack's world, my world? While I was shattered and dazed, I now admit that I was also in some measure thankful that a credentialed professional had provided us with an explanation for why Jack never seemed to outgrow the delays we had chalked up to premature birth. I also felt like I was becoming smarter, more in control. We now had direction. The fog was lifting. The diagnosis explained why back in the NICU Dr. Friedrich, with his brooding brows, would not leave Jack in peace. Our son had a syndrome, and it had a name: "Sotos."

Waking up

The label was a double-edged sword—at the same time cruel and kind. Kind because it explained the limp muscles, difficulty feeding, low tone, fast growth, and the fact that our kid was still not walking a full six months after his twin was. Cruel because it did nothing *for* Jack. Having a name for this collection of characteristics did not change anything. Jack was still the same goofy-smiled little guy we adored. A diagnosis neither erased Jack's reality nor made it worse. Today, Sotos was just another five-letter word, but what significance would this word take on over a lifetime?

It is taking me a while but I am waking up to the fact that the act of proclaiming the words, the bestowing of a label, would change nothing. My fatal flaw would be not so much the diagnosis as it would be falling prey to limiting beliefs about my son because of that diagnosis. No, my Achilles heel would be what I would allow to change or not in terms of how I viewed my child.

The limitations and leverage of measuring kids

Unless self-diagnosed, our kids' diagnoses and labels are assigned based on some form of measure—medical, psychological, intellectual, or behavioral. These tests, inventories, or surveys, whether administered in a hospital, doctor's office, therapy room, or classroom, are built to compare, benchmark, sort, and generate a label that gives "a name" to a cluster of characteristics or "indications" as they call them. In that sense, they are perfectly designed to achieve their ends. But they are no measure of a child, not by a long shot.

Labels and diagnoses at best serve a limited set of functions. As we said, they offer explanation, knowledge, and a degree of closure to what many parents describe as a frustrating and even terrifying mystery.

The irony is that a diagnosis or label means everything and nothing at the same time. It means *Everything* because it offers the explanation and personal understanding we crave. It means *Nothing* because it is just a word that serves as shorthand for a collection of other words. On its own, a diagnosis does nothing to improve life for your child, which when you get down to it is really all we parents want—a better life for our child.

What a diagnosis does is serve as a ticket. Not the "golden ticket" of Willie Wonka fame that everyone in town is clamoring for, but still a ticket. In most cases diagnosis is the price of entry to therapy, treatments, services, supports, modifications, and accommodations.

A realtor friend of mine reminds me that in her line of work it is all about "location, location, location." Similarly, in the diagnosis game it all boils down to "information, information, information." A diagnosis should inform but never drive beliefs and actions toward your child. To the extent that the diagnosis points the parent toward supports, treatment, or therapies that improve everyday functioning, it is a useful thing. When a diagnosis leads to occupational, physical, or speech therapy, sensory integration techniques, dietary changes, adaptive devices, and, yes, even medication, it can provide a vital road map to help your child.

Static diagnoses versus circumstantial labels

Carmen's child was diagnosed with autism spectrum disorder. She used the diagnosis to get her son one-to-one behavioral training, to enroll him in a social support circle, to access private therapy at a center that specializes in the anxiety profiles of autistic children. That same diagnosis allowed her to secure an individual aide on the school bus to ensure her son got safely to all his after-school therapies. Robert used his son's diagnosis of autism and Down syndrome to pay for summer camps and in-home applied behavior analysis training. In both instances these interventions improved school performance and daily living for these children. In one case these supports improved the child's behavior to the extent that he was able to thrive in a general education classroom with minimal support. In the other case it helped the child to completely shed his special education label over time. While still autistic, this boy progressed such that his diagnosis no longer impacted his school life to the point where he required ongoing special education intervention. Because educational labels are defined by the degree to which a diagnosed disability impacts learning or social interaction in the classroom, they can come and go.

Diagnoses remain, but the degree to which the diagnosis impacts an individual's daily functioning can decrease over time or fluctuate based on circumstances. For example, cognitive behavior therapies or appropriate medication can mitigate attention deficit disorder (ADD) symptoms to the point where they cannot be detected in some children in some circumstances. Technically they still have ADD, but it has minimal impact on their lived experience. Occupational therapy can provide a child with sensory integration disorder workarounds that allow a child to participate in activities with friends that had been thought impossible. The diagnosis remains but its impact is muted.

Full disclosure: I have a personal bias against the labels that emanate from diagnoses and feel that on balance they do more harm than good. However, like most forces in this world (other than Voldemort or possibly Darth Vader), they can't be boiled down to purely "good" or "evil." The diagnosis does vital work for families, and therein lies its strength and value. It is precisely their diagnosis that gives children access to timely and targeted supports and scaffolds. These supports and scaffolds ultimately offer them a seat at the table with typical peers, which opens up opportunities, broadens their tolerance of new experiences, and, in a few cases, eventually allows them to shed their educational labels. As for their diagnosis, the extent to which a child feels its impact on their school and social life can be minimized.

I know the pain of parents who feel in their gut that something is wrong and see their child struggling but who are avoiding a more primal fear: the stigma that they perceive will come with diagnoses and labels. I have been in your place. To these parents, I say get the evaluation (or allow it if the school is suggesting one), if only for the information it provides. It is your choice then regarding how or if you want to disclose a psychological or medical diagnosis, or whether to accept an educational label or not. This world is chock full of paradoxes. Here the irony is that sometimes we need the diagnosis, to beat the diagnosis into submission.

The faces of neurodivergence

Neurodivergence like eye color or hair color exists on a spectrum. We all diverge from the norm to some degree. What makes humanity interesting is that we are not trapped in some Orwellian sci-fi nightmare where everyone's the same. With ADD, dyslexia, specific learning disabilities, anxiety disorder, cognitive processing delays, and high-functioning autism spectrum disorders there are often no markers that can be readily detected by the untrained eye. They have been erroneously called silent disabilities. But of course they are not silent at all for the person living them. They scream their impact on how people experiencing them see the world, how they affect their thinking, their sensory experiences, and their relationships.

In the case of children with genetically determined syndromes such as Down, Williams, Sotos, Mafar, Prader-Willi, Malan, Rhett, and KIF5C, or those with significant intellectual impairments or neurological disorders like cerebral palsy, there are identifiable physical characteristics. They may include different facial expressions, involuntary movements or sounds, drooling, or other physiological behaviors that are out of the person's control. Here the disability is observable. I have never quite made peace with the ill-informed and insensitive comment a friend offered up, out loud to me, about my son. "All you have to do is look at him to know that something is wrong with him." Pause for jaw dropping. What? An entirely different book needs to be written to unpack all that is wrong with that comment and others like it that so many of us have endured, but it does illustrate the outsized role of appearance in society's acceptance of neurodivergence. I think of the majority culture's response this way: "Okay, have your disability but keep it pretty. The less we have to see of it, and by extension be made uncomfortable by it, the more acceptable it is." There are TV shows and movies that feature high-functioning autistics, and endearing, emotionally intuitive, and enterprising people with Down syndrome. Because for the most part that is where society's tolerance level lies.

But regardless of whether your child's disability is observable or not, he is still the same individual—the act of proclaiming the words, sprinkling diagnostic fairy dust, or bestowing of a label changes nothing. As monumental as it may seem for you, the diagnosis is a non-event for your child. They are the same person the day before the diagnosis as they are the day after. Parents, listen up here: The problem is not so much the diagnosis as it is the limitations that are assumed because of that diagnosis. It is precisely what changes (or doesn't) within us as the most influential people in our children's lives that can create seismic shifts over a lifespan. This same advice goes too for grandparents, aunts, uncles, and brothers and sisters if they have a significant role in your child's life.

Avoid self-fulfilling prophecy

The ugly underbelly of the diagnosis is how it can change us. If it kicks us, full throttle, into "sheeple" mode, if it has us resolutely buying into each prognostication associated with the diagnosis, if it causes us to become overly protective or limiting with our child, it is a problem. It has now officially crossed the line that separates what is productive from what is unproductive.

Unless we are a society that categorizes for categorization's sake, and for all our faults I believe we are not, then the only morally defensible reason for diagnosing children is the prospect that the act of diagnosis will trigger activity that improves our child's daily life. Therefore, when the diagnosis changes our behavior in negative or fear-inspired ways that limits or constricts our child's world, it is by definition doing more harm than good.

Parents of children who have been diagnosed gain nothing for their child by living in denial. The diagnosis is a thing. Proper diagnosis leads to proper treatment and support. Improper diagnosis can be damaging. For example, while growing up my son avoided eye contact like the plague. Most people assumed he was autistic. In fact this behavior stemmed from a classic stutter that was developing as a secondary characteristic of his syndrome. Assuming a diagnosis of autism would result in vastly different speech therapy treatment than a diagnosis of stuttering. Similarly, attributing your child's unrelenting protests every time he has to go on a class field trip to an anxiety disorder leads to very different treatment than attributing that same avoidance to a sensory-processing disorder. An accurate diagnosis can be a gamechanger.

However, we do need to be ever-vigilant lest we begin to swallow hook, line, and sinker every characteristic, indication, or limitation that is associated with our child's syndrome or condition.

In fact, just the opposite is true. *Our children are children first.* Each one of them is created an incalculably rich being with distinct personality, interests, and inclinations. They each have more in common with other kids than they do with a collection of possible (not even confirmed) clinical attributes. The diagnosis may label your child with learning problems, trouble relating with others, difficulty navigating reciprocal relationships, rigid thinking, lack of verbal expression, a tendency toward seizures or heart problems, etc., but their more universal label of "kid" most certainly says they are curious, less self-conscious than adults, playful, mischievous, and drawn toward whatever they consider fun. They want to laugh, they want to learn, they want to be like the adults around them, they crave new sounds, sights, and smells, they want to explore, they are loving and want to be loved. All of our kids regardless of their diagnoses share these characteristics and are united by them.

In high school when my child avoided work, took shortcuts, missed deadlines, and did the bare minimum on a collaborative history project, I was all too willing to chalk it up to the learning disabilities and cognitive processing delays associated with his syndrome. And why wouldn't I? It was all right there in his diagnosis in black and white: learning delays, lowered cognitive-processing speed, executive-functioning delays, difficulty with social relationships, etc. An open and shut case of a diagnosis predicting behavior. Or so I thought, until I learned that his neurotypical classmate, a friend's son, was having similar problems committing to the project and completing his assigned sections on time, and was turning in what my friend considered low-quality work. Maybe this boy's work avoidance, work quality, and completion issues were not at the level of my child's, but they were of the same type. I was reminded that my kid wasn't so different from the "neurotypies" all around him. If we remember that our disabled kids are kids first, we can view our child's behavior through the lens of overall child development, as opposed to giving everything to the diagnosis.

In fact, all children struggle to some extent with impulse control, want to do what they want when they want to do it, have trouble prioritizing and making choices, get distracted, and cut corners—it is part of being a kid. These same behaviors also fall into a whole suite of competencies that we lump under the term executive functioning. It is a useful exercise to remember that there are aspects associated with growing up with which all children struggle.

I do not discount serious challenges that are predicted by our child's diagnosis, such as ritualistic behavior, sensory sensitivity, hyper- or hypotonia, difficulty interpreting facial expressions, etc. This is just an important reminder that there are lots of reasons kids engage in behavior and not all of them can be tracked directly to their diagnosis. Jessica's daughter wanting to play the same Fortnite level over and over into the wee hours may be just as attributable to teenage immaturity as it is to ritual behavior indicated by her autism spectrum disorder (ASD) diagnosis. It is worth considering that sometimes our child's difficulties smack more of "kids' stuff" than elaborate manifestations of characteristics associated with their neurological condition or disability.

When we come to believe and then begin to expect to see specific characteristics or indications of our child's condition, we run the risk of manifesting that which we expect to see. This is not just New Age, mystical, conspiracy theory stuff. Researchers have been investigating the link between expectations and behavior for years.

When we use the diagnosis as a reductive explanation of everything we see within our child, when we mold our expectations to fit the diagnosis, we change our behavior toward our child and begin to see what we believe around every corner. If we *expect* our child to be distracted because they have the label ADHD, we are not surprised when they come home with only a third of their math problems complete. We say, "Of course, it is their ADHD." Whether they sense your resignation or whether the instruction they are receiving at school is just not meeting their needs, your child does less and over time confirms your belief that your kid doesn't complete work because of their ADHD; and so the cycle continues. If we expect that our child is not interested in peers because of their ASD diagnosis, we easily explain away their reason for sitting alone at the lunch table. We learn to expect it; and every time we see it, it confirms our belief that our child is not associating because of their ASD. All of this cements our belief that our child's isolation is predetermined by their diagnosis, dissuading us from looking into other factors for her isolation—aka a lack of opportunities to connect with kids with similar interests or the need for more scaffolds to help her make initial contacts, etc.

A rose by any other name

People with disabilities and those who love them are in the middle of a vibrant debate about what diagnostic information to share with children, and how and when to share that information. Remembering whence we came helps us understand where we are and why we have such strong feelings one way or another about it.

There was a time in not too distant memory when neurodiversity (and other forms of diversity) were a source of shame and those who varied from "the norm" were shut away, considered less than human. In her memoir *A Thorn in My Pocket* Temple Grandin's mother recounts the excruciating tales of being advised by doctors and cajoled by her husband to institutionalize Temple and "forget her." As recently as 1980 being stamped with such now-offensive labels as "mentally retarded," "mongoloid," and "moron" was all it took to get a person with an intellectual impairment separated from society and even sterilized. Similarly those with ASD were regularly institutionalized under the deceptive label "childhood schizophrenia."

Now unthinkable, we cringe at the inhumanity, prejudice, and short-sightedness of robbing our families of loving relationships with siblings and children, not to mention robbing society of the contribution of amazing brains who spur innovation because they think differently.

Today we recognize that "difference" does not mean "deficit." We can be proud of the fact that parents like us who have come before, as well as the self-advocates who we have raised, have been at the forefront of creating change. Today, rather than hide or look upon difference as a cause for shame, we can celebrate it.

There is a lot of positive energy among parents, particularly those of children who are on the spectrum, to educate the world about their children's diagnosis. They actively seek to tell as many people as possible about "who their child is." One parent exuded contagious glee when she shared that she wants to shout her child's diagnosis from the rooftops because she believes it will increase understanding and educate the world. Self-advocates who share their life experience on popular YouTube channels and social media accounts help normalize all manner of difference. In the media, characters like Julia on *Sesame Street* and Sam on the TV show *Atypical*, and actor Zack Gottsagen, star of the movie *The Peanut Butter Falcon*, embody this mindset. Shame can't exist in the light of day. Such efforts from movie and TV stars and everyday anti-ableism warriors have done much to scrub any remnants of shame that may exist due to neurodivergence. All this has created a more humane and tolerant world that relegates the institutional mindset that prevailed through the 1970s to being a disgraceful chapter out of ancient history that we'd prefer just to forget.

So as we continue to create a world that increasingly celebrates neurodiversity and disrupts ableism, parents are still left with the job of talking with their child about their diagnosis (or not). This is not easy. Our kids rightly have questions. The question for parents is: When and how do we answer them?

Knowledge is power

We know from our own experience that self-knowledge is good. It helps us understand ourselves and make sense of ourselves in relation to others around us. A recent experience brought this idea home to roost for me. On what I thought was going to be a comfortable jog I found myself literally sucking wind as other runners left me in the dust.

This realization was disorienting and disturbing until I recognized the fact I was running at a higher elevation than I was used to. This self-knowledge was immediately comforting to me. It helped me make sense of what I was experiencing in my body.

Similarly, for our kids who think differently, are neurodivergent, or who have disabilities, self-knowledge is healing. It gives individuals who are often made to feel helpless more power and promotes agency. I have seen it in my own son. Understanding his disability cleared up the confusion for him. It gave him an explanation for why he experienced the world differently than his friends, why he preferred certain things to others, and why some things are harder for him than for other kids.

Generally we all manage our lives better when we understand ourselves. We help our kids gain self-knowledge when we encourage them to think about how they think, move, and communicate. Meta-cognition they call it, and we all need it. The ability to consciously engage in metacognition (to think about your thinking) varies across people and disabilities. Some kids with an ASD have higher meta-cognitive abilities than their neurotypical peers, while kids with intellectual disabilities and traumatic brain injury have reduced ability to consciously think about their own thinking.

But, regardless of the degree or type of neurodivergence, increasing self-awareness improves quality of life. For some kids that might look like understanding preferences and feelings they have in their body (sometimes called interoception); for others it might be a deep understanding of how their brain approaches math tasks or why they like routines.

Empower, not enslave

We want to empower our child with self-knowledge without making them slaves to a diagnosis. Many of my middle and high school students, particularly those on the spectrum, lead with their label, even in social conversations. "Because of my autism I don't eat pizza with red sauce," "I don't like loud people because of my autism," "My ADHD makes me procrastinate." I am encouraged by these students' transparency and the self-understanding that allows them to communicate it.

But at the same time I get really worried when a diagnosis starts to sound like an excuse. I help them avoid a fixed mindset with strategies like reframing their thinking and using their own preferences and creativity to encourage growth, trading words like: "My autism makes me not comfortable in this big room" with "I am working on feeling comfortable in big rooms"; "I don't go to the basketball games because of my autism" with "I am experimenting with different kinds of earplugs because I like to support my high school basketball team"; or "My ADHD makes me turn things in late" with "Phone reminders are a tool I use to get work in on time."

It is a personal preference how we identify. I believe that we can hold two reasonable thoughts in our heads at the same time. Number one: that our neurodivergence is part of our identity and something to be understood and respected. And equally important, number two:

that we can know ourselves while maintaining a growth mindset that builds potential and doesn't allow a label to become larger than ourselves.

Holding true to both of these can be yet another difficult needle for parents to thread. It is a parent's decision when and how to talk with their child about their disability. You make these decisions based on age, what your child can understand, and what you know about how your child processes information.

JACK'S STORY

I knew my child. I was concerned that if we focused on the syndrome, Jack would cloak himself in it, use it as a crutch, to justify expecting less of himself. I worried that he would likely become fixated on the specific diagnosis words "Sotos" and "syndrome." So while we were very open about the impacts of his syndrome (low tone, decreased cognitive-processing speed, stuttering, lack of body awareness, etc.), I chose not to use the words "Sotos syndrome." We focused on what mattered to a "young" Jack rather than the "adult" label, and that was how he experienced the syndrome on a day-to-day basis, how it affected moving, eating, speaking, how it tired him out and made his muscles go limp, particularly when it was humid outside.

I did not want to unload the whole syndrome on him with its laundry list of attributes, particularly those that he was not currently experiencing. I talked with him only about those specific "indications" of the syndrome that affected him personally. We framed them as challenges to be overcome, or at worst deficits that could be improved with workarounds, rather than immutable traits that he needed to live with. These were discussed as short-term setbacks that definitely made it harder, but that could get better for him with work and practice. When we had to give "it" a name, we often called it a muscle weakness condition because it affected all his muscles globally. There were other issues around processing time and relationships, but this was the shorthand we used when he was little. Instead of saying "Your Sotos syndrome makes all your muscles weak and hypotonic and it makes you tire easily, slows down your thinking and response time, gets in the way of understandable speech, and makes it hard to make friends," we explained it as "Because of this muscle weakness condition, you are working on strengthening muscles all over your body, on balance and core strength, you are practicing holding a pencil and using your mouth and tongue muscles to make speech sounds."

I liked framing what Jack was experiencing as a "muscle weakness condition" rather than a "syndrome" because it spoke directly to what was relevant and what Jack could change through effort, and for him that was motor functioning, muscle strength, body awareness, and speech. It shifted focus off of the physical markers that figured so prominently in the syndrome but which could not be changed, like head size and shape, overgrowth, eye placement, bone age, or hand shape. These were aesthetics, and while they could make him stand out, they did not matter in the long run.

In addition to framing difficulties as challenges to be overcome or minimized with new strategies or workarounds, we spoke using strengths-based terms, identifying areas of relative strength to balance the outsized weight of weaknesses. We used strengths-based language not just for Jack but for everyone in the family. So all were used to the idea of the importance of knowing their strengths and meeting their challenges.

It broke my mama's heart when he tired and cried out, "Why are things so easy for Sammie and so hard for me?" But even these gut-wrenching times created opportunities to focus on strengths. While it may have been little comfort at the time, he heard me remind him over and over again that while he struggled with movement, he was a great reader. "There are many kids who look at a big book like you have and don't want to even pick it up, those kids struggle with reading, you are not afraid of big books."

We chose to use the term Sotos syndrome with Jack when he was older and could process the information and put the diagnosis in its proper place. Today Sotos is not an attribute he chooses to lead with, but it is also not something that he is afraid or ashamed of. For Jack, Sotos is part of his story, a small part that explains some things but that in no way defines him.

Regardless of how, when, or how often you choose to talk with your child about their diagnosis, it is important to be intentional about it. There are some guidelines which hold true regardless of your approach. These are:

- Frame challenges as opportunities for growth as opposed to fixed traits.

- Use strengths-based language and balance discussion of deficits with relative strengths.

- Focus on the characteristics of the label, condition, or syndrome that are relevant at the moment to your child in terms of improving life at home, in school, or in the community.

- Discard or minimize characteristics that your child is not experiencing, particularly those that describe physical markers that can't be altered, such as eye shape, stature, involuntary movements, etc.

- Answer all questions directly and do not avoid discussion.

- Use medical and educational diagnostic terminology with your child when they reach a developmental age where you believe they can understand and process it.

- Help your child make sense of their diagnosis and incorporate it in their own personal narrative (see Habit #11).

We want knowledge of their diagnosis to empower our child with agency and self-determination and not become recast as its own prison.

Talking with siblings

When we are raising a child with a disability or who is neurodivergent to be capable, we don't want them to fixate on labels or diagnoses. Yes they need sound knowledge about their condition and an open attitude toward discussing it, but ultimately we want them to use that knowledge to help them to get on with the business of living a meaningful life.

Similarly we want to give their brothers and sisters knowledge that helps them understand their sibling's differences, and that those differences don't change the fundamentally loving relationship they have with their brother or sister. Research confirms that children as young as two can recognize that their older brother or sister is different and can even imitate their parents' caring behavior, but still generally view their brother or sister as just "family." Somewhere in the later elementary grades children start asking questions. Older siblings can develop feelings of resentment, embarrassment, or even shame if their brother or sister's differences are called out by kids at school. The fact is even so-called "good" kids who championed their disabled sibling when they were younger can develop negative feelings as they get older if their sibling's behavior threatens to impact social standing within their peer group.

When talking with siblings, the same rules apply. Take time to point out how everyone in the family has strengths and weaknesses— that's what makes families work so well. Rochelle points out to her younger daughter Addie that while she helps her big sister Caroline who has autism calm down when she gets overwhelmed, Caroline helps her every night by going to her room with her when she gets ready for bed, because even though Addie is good at not acting out when overwhelmed, she is afraid of the dark. Regularly making these kinds of comments reminds siblings of their brother's or sister's unique strengths. Ask your children to point out what things their brother or sister is good at, to make them more aware of each other's traits. Without burdening them, show siblings how they can assist their brother or sister. Most importantly, never hide information or refuse to talk about a disability.

When talking with siblings about their brother's or sister's disability or neurodivergence:

- be honest
- decide whether or not to use diagnostic terms
- embrace questions, don't avoid them
- talk regularly about the strengths and challenges of everyone in the family
- use words that reflect a growth mindset and frame challenges as opportunities for growth
- show them how they can help each other, and that helping goes both ways!

A child is so much bigger than their label. Your child is the same kid that you love—the act of proclaiming the words, the bestowing of a label or diagnosis, changes nothing.

Put the diagnosis in its place. You had a rhythm to your life before the ground beneath your feet shook, the earth gave way, and a diagnosis was bestowed. Your child is the same beautiful quirky being you fell in love with the day they became yours. Allow your child's diagnosis to do the heavy lifting necessary to get them the help they need, but never allow it to change how you feel about your child or their potential.

REFLECT...

Consider the educational label or medical diagnosis assigned to your child. Reflect on the day when what your child was experiencing was given a "word" and ask yourself the following questions:

- What does the diagnosis or label explain?

- What knowledge does it provide?

- Where does it fall short?

- How much do you share with your child about his delays?

- Knowing your child, what information do you think is empowering, and what information do you think is unhelpful?

- Specifically, what words do you use to talk with your child?

- How might your child be motivated by greater knowledge of their diagnosis or label?

- At what age do you believe your child is best able to productively use specific information related to their diagnosis or label?

TRY IT ON...

- Make a list of the unique characteristics that you see in your child, including their special interests, personality traits, and the things that make your child who they are, including physical features if you like (e.g., contagious smile, love of animals, standing up for others, stubborn attitude, sense of humor, long eyelashes, etc.). Take your time and see how long you can get your list. Note the picture of your "whole" child that emerges.

- Once you have made the list, consider these questions:

  - Where do you see overlap with the characteristics associated with your child's diagnosis?

  - In what ways does the diagnosis fall short in describing your child?

  - How does your list compare to the generic list of characteristics offered by the diagnosis?

  - Which one better describes your child?

- Use your list to make a person word cloud that captures your child in all their complexity.[3]

- Practice using strengths-and-challenges-based language. Have everyone at the dinner table share one strength they see in a sibling or parent (you may be surprised by what you learn). Model framing weaknesses as challenges to be met, by sharing a weakness of your own, reframing it as a challenge, and describing the workarounds you have learned to manage it. When kids say "I can't" or "I am no good at...," ask them to restate what they said as a challenge to be met.

---

3   Go to https://classic.wordclouds.com for a free online word cloud generator.

Name Your Fears and Use Your Vision of Capable to Help Tame Them

HOT PINK PLASTIC POOLS

"What if he had drowned? Then what?" That was the buzz Catherine could feel coursing through Elmwood Circle cul-de-sac. It had traveled around the block and had arrived back at her doorstep via a caring neighbor: "We were all worried that Thomas would drown." Catherine admitted that her first thought was marred with more than a tinge of sarcasm: "In three inches of rainwater sitting in a toddler pool, really?" She had learned to keep these thoughts to herself.

At age seven, Catherine's second son, Thomas, was a natural swimmer, baptized again and again each summer in the cool waters off Cape Cod. He had a seal-like preference for dipping under the surface, disappearing, and coming up for air a startling distance further along the current. He could continue this rhythm in open waters for upwards of half an hour without tiring.

He was also a curious kid who would take off whenever he got the chance. "Bolting," the ABA specialist called it. And because Thomas did not communicate verbally, he typically did not let people know where exactly he was taking off to. On that particular afternoon, Thomas had spied the hot pink plastic toddler pool laid out on a sweltering concrete driveway just a few houses down. He "took off" while Catherine was distracted by his little brother and sister.

Thomas was spotted luxuriating in the cool water that had collected in the small pool and was returned home safely within 20 minutes. Those minutes when Thomas was "lost" were excruciating, but she knew the worst was yet to come. Her son could swim rings around most of the kids in the neighborhood, but still she braced for the fallout. "My fear was the judgments about what I 'should have done,' 'could have done,' or 'needed to do.'" Outwardly the sentiment from the neighbors was concern for Thomas's safety, but Catherine knew the subtext was "What is it going to take for you to keep that kid inside?" If she had more time, she would have indulged in the irony of the situation. When the kid down the street sustained a concussion in a particularly bad tackle at a middle school football game last fall she heard no collective outcry to end the boy's football career...for his "safety."

The fear she always swallowed was "Now I will have to deal with it." This insignificant incident born of childhood curiosity will be blown out of proportion, just because Thomas could not verbalize "Hey, Mrs. Giaconni, can I cool off in your hot pink plastic pool?" This would have been a non-incident if committed by another child. Catherine was afraid of how the information would be perceived, passed along, hashed over: condescension disguised as helpfulness. Irritation disguised as concern. She was not interested in more advice or commentary from people who did not know her son. Even more so she was afraid for Thomas—that he would be labeled some kind of threat. Her overarching fear was that this would be yet another strike against a whole class of humans who people are already quick to judge.

These fears simmered in a lethal stew that boiled over when Thomas "took off" again after a game at the Boston Garden, which sent bystanders and officials scanning the harbor with flashlights. During the commotion, a well-meaning friend offered a snide comment: "I guess this will be Thomas's last night in Boston." As she spoke it, fear ran its jagged nails down Catherine's insides.

Catherine had a decision to make. Was she being irresponsible? Should she keep her son home? Thomas loved nothing more than being out. That was where he experienced the world and where she learned what he loved about life.

With her decision, she sent a message to all the "well-meaners" out there, known and unknown: "You will not take away Thomas's joy, just because the situation doesn't look or feel good to you." That evening and dozens of incidents that followed steeled Catherine's resolve. She learned to ride out the snide comments and quizzical looks of folks who felt the need to limit her son to make themselves more comfortable.

Time and practice have helped Thomas learn to stay with his group. Today, whether it be on water or land, when a concerned citizen approaches to share their worry that her boy is unsafe, Catherine dismisses them with a kind but confident, "Thanks anyway. He's all set!"[1]

The Habit: Capable parents look inward and take stock of their own fears. They recognize that they need to work on themselves to ensure that their fears don't get in the way of their child's growth. They give voice to their sources of anxiety, apprehension, and agitation so they can recognize when they are reacting to their child from a place of fear rather than responding from a place of love and connection. Capable parents keep their vision for their child front and center and use that vision to manage and tame their fears.

THE SCIENCE BEHIND THE HABIT

Many people think that focusing on emotions makes us soft. Science actually proves just the opposite. When it comes to the emotions that fuel our fears, it turns out that recognizing them rather than ignoring them makes us stronger, smarter, more effective decision-makers. Labeling difficult emotions, such as fears, moves the activity away from the fight, flight, or freeze mongers that govern our lizard brain (the amygdala) to our thinking brain (the prefrontal cortex), where we can rationally consider alternatives, effectively plan, and make informed decisions.

"Name It to Tame It" is a technique pioneered by Daniel Siegel, director of the Mindful Awareness Research Center. It involves

---

1   Thomas has an autism diagnosis and is a nonverbal communicator.

noticing and labeling emotions as they're happening (Siegel 2010). "Naming" the intense emotion (saying the words out loud) has the effect of calming our revved-up nervous system—literally "taming" our brain by bathing it in a soothing neurochemical called serotonin. The result is a more relaxed state that you can actually feel in your entire body if you are paying attention.

Science has also identified two amazing side benefits to naming our intense feelings. First, doing so not only offers in-the-moment relief, but if we practice enough, we build new neural pathways that help us manage big emotions *before* we react negatively to our child. Second, when we engage in the process of naming our feelings out loud, we model managing emotions for our child. This process is called coregulating—that is, helping your child manage their nervous system as they watch and feel how you manage yours. Research shows that parents who walk through the process for themselves in view of their child also reduce their child's anxiety (National Institute for Children's Health Quality n.d.).

APPLYING THE HABIT

Amygdalas, start your engines

Parenting a neurodivergent child or one with a disability can kick our amygdala into permanent overdrive. We are confronted with a barrage of challenges on any given day, each of which threatens to confine us to our lizard brain.

You wake sleep deprived, because your child has been up and restless much of the night. You are dreading the morning routine. Will another undiscovered scratchy fabric set him off? You fret about work: you can't afford to get called away again, racing to school because of a behavior incident, your employer is losing patience. You are thrilled that your child has made so much progress handling homework demands but sense that the expectations of this new school have him close to a breaking point. The rest of the family has been begging for that long-promised vacation, but how can you book it when one kid refuses to leave his room? You tense up just thinking about it. You get a notification on your phone that the 1:1 aide is leaving. This is the second assistant who has quit this year just as your child was getting used to them. The teacher sent an email saying that your son fell asleep in the middle of math again. You silently curse not only your child's doctor but the entire medical establishment. Why can't they find the right medication? The icing on the cake, glancing at your calendar, you spy the IEP meeting scheduled for next week already convinced that the transition to middle school will trigger the painfully familiar cycle of evaluations followed by a new round of scrambling for services.

If even a fraction of this saga sounds familiar, you have been there, emotions gathering steam like the funnel cloud in *The Wizard of Oz*. You feel like lashing out at your child, the school, the doctor, the world. You contemplate escaping it all with an extended YouTube binge or another possibly more unhealthy form of self-anesthetization. Or the most merciful alternative for you may be a complete mental shutdown. This is our amygdala convincing us that our only choices are fight, flight, or freeze.

However, once the feelings are named, something happens. We are able to move them into our thinking brain (the prefrontal cortex) where we can make sense of them, prioritize concerns, problem-solve, and most importantly respond to our child in loving, helpful ways. Our fears did not disappear, they are still there. It is just that now we can respond rather than react to them.

Welcome to the emotional party

When our kids were growing up we referred to ourselves as the loud family. Everything was out there on display for everyone to see, much to the dismay of my daughters as they got older, who wished we resembled the (apparently) relaxed, Zen-like families of all their friends. Whether these families were more highly evolved or, more likely, just hid their emotions, I don't know. However, the fact is that each of us, no matter who we are, brings our own fears, past traumas, and biases to the family that we create. The temperaments to be dealt with are multiplied when grandparents, aunts and uncles, and older brothers and sisters are added to the caregiving mix. Families are teeming cesspools of emotions. How can they be anything less, when our families are often the one place where we can let down our guard and be ourselves?

Any parent who says they don't fear for their child is lying. Fear is hard-wired in us as parents. It is an evolutionary response as old as the cavemen when the terror of offspring freezing, starving, or getting eaten by wild animals drove innovation that propagated the species. Over the millennia we have replaced fears of saber tooth tigers and venomous snakes with fears of our child being rejected, made fun of, or bullied. We fear that our child will not eat enough of the right things, or will eat too much of the wrong things; that they will not work hard enough in school, or work too hard; that they will connect with the wrong crowd, or not find a crowd at all; that they will take too many risks, or not step out of their room to experience life at all.

Fear is there whether we are parenting a child who is neurotypical or neurodivergent. When our child is neurotypical, our fears hover more around "whether they will get that honor roll spot that they worked so hard for," "whether they will get the votes for the student council," "whether they will be crushed if they don't make the team or are left out by friends," or "whether they will be safe when they are driving around late at night." These fears are real, scary, and felt intensely. However, having parented neurotypical and neurodivergent children, I can argue pretty persuasively that there is a difference in quality. Just as in Dante's epic *Inferno* there are levels of angst, I believe that there is a special circle of fear reserved for those whose child is apt to be prejudged by the world based on how they look, move, communicate, think, or behave.

Below are nonexhaustive lists of "fears for my child" and "fears about my parenting" offered by parents.

Fears for my child:

- My child won't fit in.

- My child will tantrum.

- My child will be made fun of, passed over.

- My child will be ostracized, rejected.

- My child will be lonely.

- My child won't have a friend.

- My child will not learn to... (read, do math, write, walk, talk, communicate, toilet, shower, etc.).

- My child will be suspended, expelled, or kicked out of school.

- My child will not respond to a new caregiver, teacher, therapist, etc.

- My child will hurt themself.

- My child will hurt someone else.

- My child will not be able to get a job.

- My child will not be able to live independently.

- My child will not have a relationship as an adult.

- My child's medical needs will cause them pain or even death.

Fears about my parenting:

- Nothing is how it is supposed to be.

- There is a new therapy I am neglecting.

- I am engaging my child in so many therapies that he is not able to just be a kid.

- Services at the next level, school, or placement will not be good.

- I will not be able to find, travel to, or pay for the therapies, services, and/or medical procedures needed.

- I am not doing enough or I am doing too much for my child.

- I am pushing my child too hard or not pushing them hard enough.

- I will lose my temper with my child.

- Other kids in the family will miss out as we prioritize one child's needs.

- I will not be able to find a place for my child as an adult.

- My child will always live in my house.

- My child will have no place to go if I am disabled or when I pass away.

- I will lose my child or my time with them will be cut unnaturally short.

Fears named, tamed, and transformed in light of our capable vision

The cases below show how naming our fears and putting them into perspective in light of our capable vision can tame them and allow us to respond to our child in positive ways and make good decisions with and on behalf of them.

CASE #1: OBSESSED WITH "NORMAL"

I was obsessed with "normal"—whatever that is. I wanted my son "to pass." I was always scaling some mountain, where typical was the highly prized, elusive pinnacle. I imagined it there in the mist just out of reach. On park dates with friends, I avoided the sideways glances and questions about my child's "unusual" behavior. I pretended to be making small talk, you know just casually enjoying the carrots and hummus with the other parents. In reality I was hypervigilant, searching for signs of concern or confusion marring other parents' otherwise relaxed faces. I was secretly doubling as a nervous traffic cop ready to direct bystanders on, diverting questioning glances—as if to say "Move along…there is nothing to see here. This kid is just like yours."

I set up tests for my kid, many of them very public, as if other moms seeing him conquer a set of monkey bars, catching a ball, or navigating through a bounce house would come with an official certificate of approval. As if he could earn "normal" and it would be stamped on his forehead like the Good Housekeeping Seal of Approval emblazoned on a 1960s-era vacuum.

What lay behind my quest for "normal"? Why was "passing" so important? I felt like the big green Ogre in *Shrek*, needing to peel back the layers because I had created such a tough protective skin to mask my fears. For God's sake, I was a trained special education teacher, a professional advocating for the rights of underprivileged and disen-franchised children. I had numerous friends with kids with all manner of special needs. Yet I desperately did not want to identify with that for my own child.

Deep down in the crusty mantle of my being lay the source of my fears. I was afraid if people knew of my son's syndrome or detected that my child was different that he would be rejected, made fun of, or, God forbid, lonely. I feared that he would be shut off from other children who, through no merit of their own, but rather by the happy accident of having their chromosomes lined up just right, were automatically ushered into the "in group." I feared that he would not have the oppor-tunities that kids without disabilities received as a matter of course. I was afraid that if they knew of his diagnosis, or that if his way of moving, communicating, behaving, or playing lay too far out of the range of the acceptable, he would not be invited back, would be without friends, passed over for birthday parties and sleepovers, would be unable to clear the bar for inclusion in recreational sports and activities.

So great was my fear that I betrayed my own kid over and over again by putting him in uncomfortable situations where he might prove himself. I was leading with my fear.

However, once named, I could deal with my fear. I could start respond-ing rather than reacting. I now recognize that a lot of my parenting decisions were driven by my fear of Jack not passing as "normal," that he would be rejected and so would be denied entrance to many "typical" childhood rites of passage. When I looked further inward I was able to see there was a second set of tentacles to this fear that was strangling me, not as sharp as my fear for my child but still lingering, and that was the fear that people might look at me differently, ostracize me, or think me a failure. Attaching words to my fear was calming. I began to realize how exhausting and unnecessary it had been trying to put out an "acceptable" image of who my kid was—when he was amazing just as he was.

I could consider my fear in light of our shared vision of capable. It did not change my vision but it did help me clarify it. It turns out I did not want my son to be "normal." "Normal" was sloppy and inaccurate shorthand for what I really wanted, which was to raise him to be happy, strong, and able to live life on his terms.

1. *Get clear about one fear*: I am afraid that my child will be seen as too different. He has to be seen as "normal" or he will be rejected and will not have the opportunities and life choices I want him to have. By extension I will be rejected as well.

2. *Acknowledge past reaction*: I put my child through "tests," needed him to prove to others that he was "okay." I got upset if my child wanted to play in ways that might be deemed too different from other kids. I risked sending my child the message that if you are different you are not okay.

3. *Calm*: I experienced relief and began to realize how exhausting and unnecessary it was to put out an "acceptable" image of who my kid was when he was amazing just as he was.

4. *Use the vision of capable to put your fear into perspective*: By focusing on "passing" I was missing what was really important, and potentially hurting my child by forcing him to fit into an illusory notion of "typical." Understanding my fear gave me clarity on the vision. I realized that the vision wasn't for my son to "fit in," it was that he be happy, strong, and have the option to live independently.

CASE #2: IT IS A TALKING WORLD

Karissa was dead set on Brianna talking. It drove her to distraction—as distracted as a person could allow themselves to be when chasing after four kids, a baby, two girls who had autism, and a teenage brother. Brianna's big sister Miranda didn't start using words until she was almost six. Now an energetic tween, she didn't exactly sit down and have a conversation with you, but she could definitely get her thoughts across when she wanted to. Karissa had noticed how even talking a little bit had improved Miranda's relationship with extended family members and helped her fit in. Now that she was speaking in short sentences, her husband's parents would take Miranda for outings to the park and shopping. She loved the idea of her daughter bonding with her grandparents, and as a bonus their willingness to take Miranda lightened her load.

However, for her third child, Brianna, age seven already, she could hear the clock ticking. Karissa's palms became sweaty and her heart raced just thinking about it. Still she was determined Brianna would follow Miranda's lead. After all, Brianna had spoken as a toddler. Single words, but still "hi," "bye," "eat," and "more" counted as speech. Until one day her spigot of words trickled bone dry.

Since then there had been only two times when Brianna uttered a word. Once, she had jumped from her crib, busted her lip, and called "Daddy!" Karissa cursed herself for being out at the time and missing it. Then there was the time on her birthday when Karissa heard "Mommy." She cherished that one. It was the best gift she got that year or any year since.

She recalled that the doctor told them that Miranda would never talk, which made her focus on it even harder: "No one was going to tell me that my kid is not going to do something—not even a neurologist."

The fear was so sharp that Karissa's ears were always pricked. She was hypervigilant, determined not to miss an utterance when it happened. Sometimes she listened so hard that she imagined she might make it happen by sheer force of will. Karissa was adamant her daughter needed to speak because, as she said, "Brianna needed to make her way in a 'talking' world."

Brianna was her "swing, sand, swim" child who could content herself rotating between those three pursuits all day. But her behavior was getting worse. Despite the simple signs she had taught her, Brianna would flop to the ground in frustration if Karissa could not decipher from her frenetic pointing what she wanted from the top of the refrigerator. Brianna loved people, and her way of letting them know was to run and press her face against theirs and shake her head back and forth as if to say "I am so excited and pleased to meet you." That unusual sign of affection put her grandparents off. They were uncomfortable with her unpredictable behavior. It was too fast, too sharp, too unannounced. Karissa knew that if Brianna just started talking her grandparents would relax and see what she saw in her daughter. Then Brianna could have a relationship with them like her big sister Miranda had. Brianna would love nothing more than to play in the sand at the park with her grandpa, but she was not included.

The unfairness of it all had Karissa at a boiling point over Brianna's language. She alternated between crying because she could not make it better for her little girl and becoming impatient with her tantruming. She hated that her daughter was being judged as "less than" by her grandparents. Karissa knew how smart her daughter was, she understood everything, why would she just not say something...anything!

Naming her real fear opened things up for Karissa. She explains it like this: "Once I recognized I was confusing the act of talking with acceptance, I could name my real fear—that my daughter would never have the relationships that her sister has. That calmed my nervous system and opened my mind to other options for Brianna to get her 'voice' and personality into the world. I still hold out hope that she will speak, but now more than mere words, I want her to have a way to be understood and connect with family and the big wide world around her."

1. *Get clear about one fear*: I was afraid that my child would never talk and that no one would know what a bright girl she is. My

fear really was that she would be excluded, not accepted. I catastrophized that if she could be shunned by her own grandparents she could be shunned by "the world."

2. *Acknowledge past reaction*: I became emotional, breaking into tears. I felt like a failure because I could not make it better for her. I led with my fear when making decisions, avoiding visits to the grandparents' house because I felt they did not tolerate Brianna's behavior and treated her differently than her "speaking" sisters. Without knowing I was, I began getting impatient and resentful that Brianna was not on my timeline for talking.

3. *Calm*: Immediate relief, as I realized that I was stuck on verbal as the only way my daughter could get her ideas across.

4. *Use the vision of capable to put your fear into perspective*: I realized that my vision wasn't for Brianna to talk, as much as it was for her to have a reliable way to get her voice into the world, so that she would not be frustrated, and so that other people (including her grandparents) would understand what a smart, loving person she was.

The first case focuses on the desperation that comes with wanting your child to "fit in," and the second case focuses on what I call one of the "nevers": my child will never walk, talk, graduate, read, write, toilet, make a friend...fill in the blank with your own personal never. In our lizard brain we catastrophize and flee to the nevers. In both cases, once parents did the work to understand and name their underlying fear, they boiled down to fear about their child being accepted and known. As long as our amygdala is on fire, we flee to extremes—"things have to be this way or the worst will happen." Naming our fear allows our nervous system to calm down enough to put our thinking brain back in the driver's seat so that we can return to the vision of capable we have for and with our child.

Taming fears opens opportunities

A world where judging, sorting, and categorizing rules the day can be a scary place for our child to inhabit. Putting your child in a Michelin Man suit to protect them from novel or challenging situations may avoid triggering your own fears, but it will also rob your child of the experiences they need to grow and view themselves as capable. Witnessing your child being ignored or made fun of is heart-rending and automatically makes us want to indulge our most protective instincts. It is at those moments that we need to be intentional in staring down our fears, willing ourselves not to give in to them, so that we don't run the risk of limiting our child's natural growth.

These are the kinds of fears that if left unchecked result in us opting out of opportunities, avoiding new situations, and denying our child potentially enriching experiences. When we lead with our fear, we are not enabling our child to live their best life. If you are "all in" on the vision, it will help you put your fear into perspective. For example:

If the vision of capable I have with my child is that they will join with other young people to participate in a county fair because they love animals, then I need to increase her opportunities to tolerate and enjoy being around other children. That means I have to name my own anxiety around her putting her jacket on backwards with the hoodie covering her face and tame it. Given the county fair vision it is now more important to pursue opportunities that support her in being with other kids than it is to avoid the possibility of potentially embarrassing moments.

Or:

If my child's vision of capable is that he is able to attend classmates' birthday parties without getting overstimulated and tantruming, I need to recognize my fear and identify situations that lead to tantrums, without surrendering to that anxiety and creating excuses to skip parties.

Or:

> If my child's vision of capable is that he will work at the ice cream shop that he loves, I have to stare down my fear that he may be teased by another employee for having his apron tied wrong. While no one wants their child to be the butt of a joke, I have to reconcile myself to the fact that I can't control other people's reactions and that the goal of meaningful work trumps any fears I may have about my child getting made fun of.

Once we step back and play out the scenarios in our thinking brains, we see that our worries are not worth abandoning or compromising that vision. We realize that we are not alone, that we are all terrified, and yet we move forward.

If we are not intentional in naming our fears and putting them into perspective in light of our vision of capable, we run the very real risk of transferring them to our child. Our children are very intuitive; even if they can't say so they feel our anxieties very acutely. One area that parents say is universally anxiety-provoking is bullying. While kids who appear "different" are targeted by bullies more than "neurotypical kids," it is not a foregone conclusion that your child will be bullied. Parents who have a fear of bullying or who insist that their child is being bullied often encourage an unnecessary fear within their child. Research has confirmed that the more anxious you are about your child being targeted, the more anxious the child will be. Experts recommend that, instead of fanning flames around bullying, you talk with your child about the positives of staying engaged: "Think about the fun of going back to school, exciting learning challenges, interesting extracurricular activities [or whatever it is that your child really enjoys]." Parents who moderate their concerns raise children who can moderate theirs.

Staring down our fears requires strength and requires taking a risk—for us and for our child. Remember there is dignity in risk. The alternative: if we remain cloaked in our fears, we avoid the potential of unpleasantness but our child misses potentially enriching opportunities that can open their worlds and move them closer to their visions.

In the words of a popular song by Zach Williams, "fear he is a liar." Fear can talk you into all kinds of can'ts: "My kid can't go to birthday parties," "My kid can't be around all that sugar," "My kid can't wait with the other kids after school," "My kid can't be assigned a different 1:1 aide," "My kid can't go to after-school care with all those kids he doesn't know."

For me, once I had named my fear, it was helpful to imagine the worst-case scenario and then consider what my child stood to gain from reaching toward our capable vision. From that vantage point my fears seemed pretty insignificant.

"If it means my daughter is going to eat in the cafe, be part of the class, participate in robotics, get the joy of running with the cross country team, I can handle any anxiety that I might feel from a couple of sideways looks, snide comments, an awkward situation, or even a tantrum. As long as I keep my eye on the vision I can outlast any naysayers."

REFLECT...

- What are your worst fears and best hopes for your child?

- What is the source of those fears? What is the source of your hopes?

- What is the worst thing that could happen if your fears were realized?

- What is your child missing in order to keep him "safe" from the fears you imagine?

- What makes you fearful for your child?

- What do you imagine would happen if one of those fearful situations occurred?

- What would be the consequences for you? For your child?

- In what ways (subtle or otherwise) might you be transferring your fears to your child?

TRY IT ON...

- Hold one fear up against your vision of capable for your child. Isolate a fear that you have: "My child will be left out," "My child will never live independently," "My child will never have a significant friendship." Test the veracity of that fear against your shared vision.

  a. *Get clear about one fear:* Name it out loud. Notice what happens in your body when you put it into words.

  b. *Acknowledge past reaction:* How have you reacted in the past when you are met with this fear?

  c. *Calm:* Once you have named your fear, you are able to calm your nervous system and think clearly. You can now consider your fear through the lens of the vision of capable you have created with your child.

  d. *Use the vision of capable to put your fear into perspective:* Ask yourself: What could happen if that vision is realized? How does this fear potentially impact the vision?

- Give your child an opportunity that requires you to face your fear. There may be bumps, it may be complicated the first time you try, but in staring down your fears you are on the path to helping your child live their best life.

Send Capable Messages: Use Words and Act in Ways that Let Your Child Know that You Think They Are Capable

SURF'S UP, DUDE

A lifelong athlete, Kim is not a fan of the "every kid gets a trophy" philosophy. She regularly reminds her son that it is okay to fail. At the same time, she sees herself as Ryan's biggest cheerleader. Thanks to hypertonia, hypermobile joints, poor depth perception, and a shaky sense of balance Ryan has struggled with all things athletic.

Attempts to run went something like this: He would take off and before long his joints would begin to wobble, slack muscles tiring, his balance compromised due to a brain that failed to send signals to his body about how the pavement was changing under his feet. The typical result was Ryan collapsing in a heap. "Gravitationally challenged" they playfully called it.

There were so many spills and missteps that she and Ryan even developed their own secret sign. "We would lock our pinky fingers together and count '1...2...3...break,' at which point we would unlock our fingers with attitude, signaling that he was ready to give it another go."

When she booked their Hawaiian vacation, pedaling away on a bicycle or jumping into a pool were still gargantuan feats for 11-year-old Ryan. Despite these obstacles, Kim wanted her son to experience all that Maui had to offer on land and sea, and in Hawaii that included surfing.

First, she reduced the sizable balance risk that comes with surfing by replacing the standard issue surfboard with a stand-up paddleboard, which is much less likely to topple its rider. Equipment solved. The next hurdle was getting Ryan into a wetsuit and lifejacket. Then came coaxing him onto the paddleboard on his hands and knees...on land. Finally, they progressed to shallow water, Kim holding the board and walking it parallel to the shore. Each time Ryan was foiled by slack muscles or stymied by anxiety, Kim gave him a high-five for trying.

At one point an overwhelmed and waterlogged Ryan retreated to the safety of the sandy beach. Ryan knew that his mom was okay with him stepping away from their surfing mission whenever he needed to.

Before long he caught his breath, and after they exchanged a determined "1...2...3...break!" he was back in the water on his board with his mom at his side. It was then that Kim eyed a modest swell emerging in the distance. At just the right moment she turned the board toward shore and gave Ryan a push, both of them ecstatic as he rode the wave all the way in.

That is how the remainder of the day was spent, riding wave after wave as the sun lowered, surf bums and passersby cheering and knuckle-bumping Ryan each time he glided to the foamy shore.[1]

The Habit: Capable parents know the power our words and behavior have on our children. They are intentional about using words and acting in ways that send their child the message that they think he or she is capable. They are also aware that they are sending their child a message in what they don't say and in the actions they fail to take. Because it is harder to undo a negative message, capable parents err on the side of letting their child know they believe they *can* even sometimes before they are 100% sure themselves.

1   Ryan is autistic.

THE SCIENCE BEHIND THE HABIT

Why do the messages we send our kids matter so much? Well, because of some pretty basic science. The fact that what caregivers think affects behavior has been proven over and over again, but it all started in the 1960s with a particularly tenacious group of graduate students who spent a lot of time with rats.

What can parenting possibly have to do with rodents? As it turns out, a lot. This study was the first to prove that what researchers *believed* about rats affected something concrete: the rats' behavior. At first blush, it sounds far-fetched that a person's thoughts could affect the behavior of a separate, unconnected being. But it turns out this wasn't some hocus-pocus, spoon-bending sideshow, rather it revealed a basic truth that is at the same time profound and intuitive. This is how it went down: Scientists assigned each of their research assistants to care for their very own rat. Half of the group were told that they had received a "smart" rat. The other half were told that they had received a "dumb" rat. Those who believed their rats were smart petted them more, talked to them in a positive tone, and treated them more gently than the research assistants who believed they were in charge of "dumb" rats.

These differences in caregiver beliefs translated to their behavior toward their rats and actually increased the "smart" rats' ability to run mazes and effectively find food—arguably the most important skills if you happen to be a rat. Of course, in reality, these maze-winning, food-finding rats had no more natural ability than any other—they were all just rats. The only explanation for the high performance of the rats labeled "smart" was found in the pattern of consistent messages they received from the words and behavior of their caregivers (Rosenthal and Fode 1963).

So, the science follows, if we *believe* our kids are bright and capable, we will *behave* as if they are, and as a result their performance will improve. These results are not confined to rats; numerous studies have been conducted in classrooms showing that a teacher's beliefs about their students actually increased those students' performance.

This research has been the foundation of training generations of educators to maintain high expectations for all students, particularly students of color and those in poverty. If it is important for teachers to believe children can, how much more important is it for parents, who literally breathe their lifeblood into their offspring?

What is in a word?

If Habit #1 "Believe that Effort Creates Ability" is the foundation, then Habit #6 "Use Words and Act in Ways that Send Your Child the Message that You Think They Are Capable" is the fuel that feeds the engine.

What is in a word? A lot, it turns out, and there is even more punch packed into each of our words when we consider the impact of our tone of voice on children. Our children construct meaning from the tone we use when we speak, well before they understand our words (Fernald 1993).

Intriguing for everyone with kids, but for those of us raising a child with a disability, this research should give us real pause. If babies as young as 14 months are tracking what their parents say, particularly their tone of voice, what are older children tracking, even if they don't have the means to tell you what they are hearing? Don't be fooled into thinking children who are less communicative are not absorbing, if not every word, at least our tone of voice and nervous system state, because they are. Children with communication disorders, particularly kids with fewer gaze shifts, less joint attention, those who don't look you in the eye, don't communicate verbally, and those with repetitive or ritualistic behaviors, are still absorbing our words and behavior at some level.

APPLYING THE HABIT

Actions speak even louder

What messages was Kim sending Ryan each step of the way? Let's look at the messages she was putting out to her son when she bought him the wetsuit, rented the paddle board, spent her time practicing over and over again first on land, then shallow water, and finally in the waves. Ryan was likely thinking, "My mom, the person who knows me best in the world, would not spend all this money and time if she did not think I could do this. She must think I can, so maybe I can."

Safety, scaffolding, and patience

Capable parents do not let their goal of helping their child see himself as capable get in the way of good sense. We don't put our children in risky situations. Kim provided scaffolding and patience and even a safety valve for her son.

So, it is good to let your child know that you think they are capable, but is there such a thing as too much of a good thing? Can a parent go too far with this "I believe you got this" approach to parenting? The answer is that you are always better off sending positive messages because, even if your child does not get all the way there, they will end up in a better place than if you conveyed that you believed they were incapable and therefore shouldn't even bother trying.

I did not always play it safe, but thankfully my child says he has forgiven me. In my zest to help my son believe he was strong and capable, I had him carry in the milk for our family of six. I so wanted him to get the message that I believed he could do it, that optimistic zeal outweighed good sense. I intentionally gave him a gallon in each hand hoping to balance the weight. Walking ahead of him with an armload of bags, I didn't turn around to check on him so great was my desire for him to see that I believed he could. All was well, until splat! I spied a river of white was running down the asphalt cracks and past me. My son was devastated. Much later with the perspective that only time provides we had a lot of fun talking about how this was a real life "don't cry over spilt milk" moment, but at the time I just felt bad. Had I gone too far, was he really not able? In trying to show him that he could and give him strength training, motor planning, and balance practice, I risked reinforcing failure. Maybe, but once I swept the milky river off the concrete and onto the grassy banks, I acknowledged that while I would offer more scaffolds next time, I would do it all over again if my son might get those jugs even close to the kitchen counter, showing him that his parents think he can!

Not many parents would go to the lengths that Paulette Kish did, but the story of her son Daniel illustrates in living color how messages impact our kids. In 1968, at only 13 months, Daniel lost both of his eyes due to cancer. As Daniel tells it, his mother made the decision to treat him as if he was a regular kid. He was a curious little guy who loved to climb. He started by scaling the sides of his crib until he fell out and landed on the floor. When he climbed, his mother's reaction was to let him keep climbing. When he set out to explore first his house and then his neighborhood, she let him explore. When he mounted a bike and kept on pedaling down the street until he ran into a steel pole, her reaction was to let him keep riding. Over a bruising and eventful childhood, it came to pass that Daniel was a blind boy who rode a bike, navigating through town on his own, using a tongue-clicking technique he developed that uses echolocation. Now an adult, Daniel guides sighted hikers through dense forests. Literally, the blind leading the sighted! Daniel attributes much of his extraordinary story to his mom's beliefs about him and the actions that she took that reinforced her belief that he could move through the world on his own (May 2015).

Unintended messages

To what extent are our kids getting messages we don't want them to get? Even when you think your kid is not listening, they are. Sometimes our children are so absorbed in their own worlds that our heads could fall off and roll onto the floor in front of them and they wouldn't shift their gaze from their screen or turn away from their toy. We would swear it doesn't matter what we say. Even so, messages are being transmitted and they are getting them. Children are extremely intuitive, particularly our children who are neurodivergent.

Tonia and Kareem had two beautiful boys, Davean aged 12 and Jamal aged 10. Based on his unresponsive behavior his parents were convinced that Davean was wholly absorbed in his intense interests and meticulous collections. Their younger son Jamal was bright, responsive, and fully engaged in family life. Their apartment was not large. Partly out of necessity and partly because they assumed he was tuned out they had become accustomed over time to talking about the boys while Davean was in the room. After all, there was no place for him to go and he was not really listening. So they thought.

Until one day seemingly out of nowhere a frustrated Davean shed real tears. Through his cries Tonia heard Davean repeat in measured monotone syllables: "I–want–to–be–Jam–al, I–want–to–be–Jam–al." At that moment she realized that Davean had been taking in all her and her husband's conversations and was likely reacting to their words.

In other cases, without thinking, we pass messages along to our child that reflect our own difficulties and past traumas. The mom of one of my students came to me honestly expressing her frustration with online instruction during the Covid pandemic. She entered my classroom and said: "The problem is Samuel really has a hard time with the computer, he really gets anxious about using the computer, he really doesn't like getting online, he is really not good with computers..." The problem in the moment was that Samuel was standing right next to her as she spoke. I'll wager that if Samuel didn't have a problem with technology before, he was likely to question his competence after that exchange.

The messages transmitted by what we don't say can be just as powerful as those carried by what we do say. None of us are immune to it. Unfortunately, I have found myself on the sending end of such silent unintended messages more than once. When my twins were in middle school, the eighth grade was offered an enrichment project. It was aptly named the "passion project." Kids were to research a topic they were into and share with the class a report or demonstration. But Jack was painfully behind in school. He was not turning in work; he was saying he didn't care about school and was generally stressed out about all things academic. I caught myself brainstorming with his twin sister about the project, imagining with her all the directions in which she could take her chosen topic, "women in soccer." What I was doing at the same time was *not* talking with Jack about what he wanted to do, not musing a project plan with him. I stayed quiet, because I was secretly afraid that adding yet another demand, one more project, would only compound his angst around school demands, which were becoming increasingly intolerable for him. What message did Jack take from my silence around the passion project? I hope it did not come through as "I am so incompetent that I am not worthy or capable of indulging in fun activities like a 'passion project.'"

REFLECT...

- How do I communicate to my child that I believe they are capable?
- What specific words and/or actions do I use?
- What messages do I send that communicate otherwise?
- What is my vision with and for my child?
- Think about the decisions, small and large, along the way that support that vision and the words and actions that support those decisions.
- How might I change the messages I send my child?

TRY IT ON...

- Keep a journal on paper or on your phone for a couple of weeks. Note the things you say to your child (including those that you say within earshot of your child) as well as the way you behave toward your child. If you have a partner, review each other's journals. Review your journal(s) in light of the questions above.
- Try on specific language with your child that tells them they

can do something even if you have not seen them do it yet and/or you are not sure that they can do it. Some examples:

- "You love fairies, I know you can draw one."

- "You love the *Star Wars* theme, I know you can brush your teeth for the whole song."

- "Now that you have that new regrouping strategy down, I know you can finish that whole math practice page."

- "You showed me that you know how it feels in your stomach when you have to go to the bathroom, I bet you can do it again today or tomorrow."

Set the Expectation that Others Treat Your Child as Capable

Sometimes but I don't like when my dog begs for food. My dog can do tricks he sits he stays he comes he lays down he can also act like a circus dog.

So large and bold was the font that those two run-on sentences nearly filled the 8 by 11 page. Di's eyes widened as she scanned the "essay" that Phineas, her 16-year-old, handed her.

Diane, an English teacher by trade, shook her head in disbelief. Was she just romanticizing the past? Phineas may not have loved traditional school subjects, but up through grade school he was writing, really writing. In third grade, his teachers began expecting him to compose three-paragraph essays and, with the support of the paraprofessional assigned to the class, he did! She recalled a particular essay describing a family trip to Lake Samish from when Phineas was 11. No, she was not revising history. That essay was an actual story, complete with a main idea, supporting details, and even dialog.

She knew Phineas could do better because she had seen him do it, but apparently his teachers in the high school life skills classroom did not.

She sat Phineas down that night and repeated the essay prompt: "Describe a time when you taught a person or a pet something new." This is the task you were assigned, Diane said. She got her son talking, transcribing his thoughts, requiring him to supply specific details when he offered generalities. Finally she had Phineas read over the draft and make edits. The next morning Phineas turned in this new three-paragraph essay in exchange for the two sentences he had produced the day before.

Diane asked that Phineas be moved to another English class. She wanted teachers who would challenge her son and not let him off the hook with what she considered "lazy" answers. That year Phineas was transferred to a classroom where the adults expected him to read, make inferences about what he read, think, revise his thinking, and write real essays.[1]

The Habit: Capable parents set the expectation that others treat their child as capable. They know that as important as they are, parents cannot, should not, and definitely will not be the only influences in their child's life. Habit #6 spoke to the power of the messages that we send our child. Habit #7 explores how we set the same bar for strangers, helpers, and professionals in our child's orbit.

THE SCIENCE BEHIND THE HABIT

There is an extensive body of research and even a name for the kind of helping that hurts. It is called learned helplessness. Learned helplessness is defined as not acting, or limiting your action(s), because you have come to believe that you can't do something or that whatever you do will not make a difference. Science shows that when people believe they can't or believe what they do doesn't matter, they stop doing.

Independence among young adults and adults who are neurodivergent depends on a range of factors, including degree of disability, family situation, and availability of community-based residential options. The research is not conclusive, but the statistics are startling. Seventy percent of adults with disabilities live with their parents

1   Phineas is diagnosed with autism spectrum disorder.

instead of in more independent living situations (Newman *et al.* 2011). We can't say the degree to which learned helplessness has a part to play. But suffice it to say, the more we raise our kids to see themselves as capable, the less they will find themselves trapped in unwanted cycles of dependency.

APPLYING THE HABIT

Well-meaners, do-gooders, and saviors

When it comes to our kids and the people in their orbit, there are personality types that can get in the way. I call them the well-meaners, the do-gooders, and the saviors. The world is filled with them, the serial helpers, safety bees, and people who are just plain uncomfortable with children and adults who register to them as "different." Granted there may be a reasonable explanation to each of these folks' motivations. The motivation for the serial helper is compassion. The safety bee avoids danger. Even those who approach people who are "different" with skepticism are activating a primitive protective response within themselves.

From the perspective of the doer, this is all perfectly rational behavior. But if you are raising your child to be capable, this behavior is worse than unhelpful, and could even cause damage, especially if your child is exposed to it systematically over time.

This is not to say that all that helping is bad. Humans are an obliging species. We see someone who we judge to be having a hard time and we want to make it easier for them. This noble human emotion spurs us to open the door for the elderly, to grab the elbow of a person with a visual impairment, or to reach an item off the high shelf at the grocery store for someone using a wheelchair. There is nothing wrong with offering a helping hand. Such gestures are a hallmark of our humanity. They connect us as brethren on this planet, one to another.

Polite offers of help are just that, polite offers, as long as we have the option to respond with an equally polite "No thanks" should we choose. The ability to say "No thanks" is something that most of us never give a second thought. However, those two words are not taken for granted within the disability community. In fact, being able to make these kinds of simple choices is a big part of what is called "agency"—that is, the ability to impact your own environment. Helping becomes a self-reinforcing quagmire when a person doesn't have the "agency" or loses the will to say "No thanks."

Too often children and young adults who don't communicate verbally, or who can't or don't reliably turn down help, experience a barrage of others offering, filling in gaps, finishing sentences, supplying items, making choices, and completing steps for them. These helpers assume our children can't hear, can't reach, can't choose, can't lift. Can't, can't, can't. The cycle is self-reinforcing because, over time, children, teens, and even adults on the receiving end of this "help" come to believe that they "can't" or are not "able." Or they figure, "Why should I try if someone is going to do it (or redo it) for me anyway?"

Some may say, "Wait a minute, there are things that I don't attempt to do, and as a result someone else does them for me—and I don't have learned helplessness." True. Evidence, the dance that happens between couples when one pretends they don't know where the gas pump is inserted and another feigns being completely baffled by laundry to avoid these tasks. Most of us can recognize ourselves in harmless interpersonal farces like the one described. The difference, in these cases, is that there *is* agency—we are choosing to ignore something in an effort to get someone else to act on our behalf. (And that is a completely different problem for a completely different book.)

We need to be concerned about the truly crippling phenomenon that is prevalent within communities that have been judged as "different," and be on the lookout for signs of it in our children.

Legitimate supports

Don't confuse legitimate support and scaffolds that are intended to "level the playing field" for our children with disabilities with learned helplessness. There is a subtle but critical distinction between life-enhancing supports that children with disabilities and many who are neurodivergent require and what they have been *conditioned to think they require.*

There are many personal care, academic, and physical tasks for which our children need support and accommodations to complete. For example, a pencil grip may be a support that allows a child with motor impairment to write. However, employing a human scribe for every assignment regardless of length may send a child the message that someone is going to write for them, so why try. Using the Natural Reader app to decode words on difficult reading passages may help a child with dyslexia better answer comprehension questions, but using Natural Reader for all reading assignments may result in a child giving up trying to read. Giving a child a picture schedule may help him independently complete his shower routine, but showering him every day to make sure he does not miss a step in the process tells him that adults are going to wash me anyway, so why bother?

Each of us, whether disabled or not, as the song says, "get by with a little help from our friends," and there is absolutely nothing wrong with that. The key is that the help has the intention of *empowering* not doing for a person so they don't make mistakes, take too long, make a mess, or do a task in a way that others don't approve of.

Setting the tone with Jack's helpers

I feared that Jack would be helped too much and would begin to believe the negatively seductive lies behind the kind gestures: "I can't do this, I can't do that—but someone else will do it for me."

We can make the mistake of assuming that learned helplessness is a blight reserved mostly for individuals whose movement is severely impaired, those without a reliable form of communication or who are severely sensory impaired. This is not so. My son wasn't in a wheelchair, he wasn't nonverbal or blind. Yet I had seen the negative effects of well-meaners overhelping, and was hyperaware of making sure that the insidious effects of learned helplessness were not creeping in and choking off his choices and agency, shaping a view of himself as incapable.

I had my "well-meaner radar" up, and so did not encounter too many problems with close friends or family imposing their help or limiting choices for Jack. They took their cues from me, they knew Jack's mama and trusted me (at least at some level). Even if they wanted to help, ease what they saw as a burden, or make things more comfortable for Jack, they followed the leader, at least in my presence.

While I am sure that my behavior prompted more than a few raised eyebrows, the owners of those perplexed brows took their lead from me. If I let Jack struggle an uncomfortably long time to push the plastic straw into his juice box, or allowed Jack to teeter on unsteady legs across uneven surfaces, they cringingly allowed it. When I handed him an obviously too-heavy cooler or tote bag full of park paraphernalia and walked away, with Jack groaning, family and friends scratched their heads and assumed, "I guess she knows what she is doing."

Those close to us soon learned if they tried to step in and make things easier or "safer" for Jack, they pretty quickly encountered a resolute look from me or were interrupted with a "He's got that."

Our situation may have appeared a little curious at times but, I reminded myself, it was nothing compared to what Daniel Kish's mom must have experienced. Imagine how many well-meaning safety hawks she had to dismiss as she allowed her blind son to get around on that bicycle!

The real landmines lay in situations where I was not present, in the great beyond where I, as mom, did not wield absolute power.

I was concerned with the places where I wasn't. As Jack grew, the helpers and well-meaners would begin to move in, occupying the spaces where I was not involved to mediate expectations. All of these people with the ostensibly positive motive of making something easier for my son. These were good people, trusted babysitters, teachers, scout leaders, and other parents who became uncomfortable seeing Jack struggle. They saw him navigating the room, bearings awkward, arms out at half guard; they saw him topple over, they saw him tiring, fatigued by the work of moving his body through space. These "first responders" predictably came to the rescue.

I began to see the helpers and do-gooders move in, all with the ostensibly positive motive of making something easier for my son.

This pattern of underestimating reared its ugly head throughout Jack's childhood. People would make decisions for my kid. Scout leaders seeing a knot-tying or cooking task that they judged to be too challenging and not giving him the option to say "No thanks, I want to try this myself." Teachers serving up easier low-level "yes–no" questions, letting him off the hook for not responding if he did not get the answer out immediately. When making Mother's Day gifts, after-school monitors cutting out pieces for him, to save him from having to manipulate the "dangerous" scissors. PE teachers, looking the other way, allowing Jack to sit out or quit early.

In all these cases, others made decisions for Jack or let him opt out, in effect taking away opportunities to try, struggle, learn, and feel a sense of accomplishment. Even if it is just the dignity that comes with knowing you cut out and attached the antler on the reindeer picture yourself...no matter that they are a little crooked and look more like two cauliflower than six-pointed racks—you did it!

Three types of helpers

As the most influential people in our child's life, the messages we send about their competence carry the most weight. But we are not the only ones contributing to building our child's sense of who they are. It is just as important that those people who our child encounters every day treat them as capable.

Over the years I have identified three types of "others" that your child meets every day. They are the strangers, regular interactors, and the professionals. Whether knowingly or not each has a role to play in helping your child believe they are capable.

Strangers

This is the guy in the grocery store who jumps in and grabs the item off the shelf, because your child or young adult has movement impairments and is taking longer to reach up and grasp the desired item off the high shelf. You cannot always control strangers, and as your child grows you are not always there to jump in and set or model that expectation.

The best way to address strangers is with a polite "He's got that, no worries!"; and when they are able, teach your child to do the same. You are never going to reach them all and it is not your job to do so. But, who knows? As you set the tone for how you want your own child treated, a few of these overly zealous helpers may actually stop and think twice next time before jumping in.

Regular interactors

These are the army of people that your child interacts with on a regular basis at school, in after-school activities, or in their adult program or at work. They include the bus driver, cafeteria staff, after-school monitors, friends' parents, coworkers, bosses, etc.

TYLER AND THE HALF-EATEN SANDWICH

Tyler preferred to dine leisurely rather than scoff down his lunch like the other teenage boys. Food just was not a big motivator for him. Without prompting he might "graze" over the contents of his lunch box for upwards of an hour. It was during a casual conversation with Tyler's mom Sharon that the bus driver offered that Tyler had not been in the van for any of the transition program's community outings for over a month. Sharon was further shocked when she learned that the van driver had determined that Tyler was "better off" staying back and finishing his lunch and so he would not have to be hustled to pack up his half-eaten sandwich and rush to board the nine-passenger van for community training. Sharon talked to aides and the van driver and made sure that it was written in the communication book that Tyler would attend community training with his peers whether or not he finished his sandwich when it was time for the bus to leave.

Communicate your expectations clearly and in writing if necessary to all the people who regularly interact with your child. Share with cafeteria workers, library staff, and bus drivers the vision you have developed with your child. "It is really important Samantha takes the time to pick her lunch even if it takes a little longer." "We are teaching responsibility so if she spills, she knows she should clean it up, so it is important for you to ask her to do so."

Professionals

These are the pros in your child's life: the practitioners, the trained teachers, aides, therapists, and even doctors.

WHOSE FAVORITE IS IT REALLY?

As 16-year-old Haley sat in her inclusive English class, Ms. Simone, the teaching assistant, read test questions to her. It would have taken longer, but Haley could have read them herself. Ms. Simone knew Haley well after working with her for almost two years. In fact she knew her so well that she occasionally jumped in suggesting responses that she thought Haley might be thinking. When it was time for the writing portion of the test, Ms. Simone read the prompt: "Describe your favorite game including how you would teach someone else to play." While Haley began to process the question, Ms. Simone cheerfully supplied, "Oh, Haley, this is an easy one, you always play Uno...write about that one." Haley complied and Ms. Simone and she proceeded with the essay. Later when asked about how she felt about the test, Haley said, "I have so many games I like, I was just deciding which one to pick, I love playing Jenga with my brother, but Ms. Simone told me to write about Uno, so I wrote about Uno."

Shockingly, in small bites, well-intentioned overhelpers can even eat away at our child's agency over their own preferences. Here too it is important to communicate your expectations clearly and in writing. This is where the IEP is your friend as professionals are accustomed to implementing what is prescribed in IEPs and using them for guidance when they are unsure of what to do. Ensure that the vision of capable and your expectations for getting there are written directly into your child's IEP. "We prefer that Haley has time to process and formulate responses before suggestions or narrowed choices are offered." In addition, remind providers of your intentions and model them when you are together in IEP meetings and other settings. If you want others to give your child extra processing time before jumping in, make sure that you are allowing your child to formulate their ideas and are not supplying answers for them.

There is no doubt that the professionals who work with your child have skills that you do not. They are experts in their field and have training in child development, learning theory, brain science, movement, and speech theory, and they apply all of this knowledge on behalf of children. But remember you remain the *expert in your child*. Let them know your perspective based on your experience with your child.

As important as sharing your perspectives is, it is more important to empower your child to communicate their preferences; teaching them to say "Wait, I need more time" or "No worries, I have got this," whether that be through spoken means, signing, or an assistive device.

Changing minds one interaction at a time

A school lunch lady said this after she read my previous book *Capable*: "Now when the kids from the self-contained or supported classrooms come through, I don't automatically set their milk on their tray and load up their lunch—I step back and see what they can do before I reach in. I have been surprised with how independent the child can be, and I now see that my overhelping, jumping in, and loading up their trays was unnecessary and not helpful in the long run."

Further showing how we set the tone with others around us, I had a parent who was also a friend say the following: "I knew there was something going on with Jack, but you always treated him as if he could—so I took my cues from you." I wore this like a badge of honor because I saw it as evidence that my message was getting through. Other people don't know what your child can do, but when they see you expecting your child to engage in or at least try certain things, they believe it is okay for them to expect the same. If others do not have the opportunity to *see* what you expect of your child, tell them. Let them know what your child is doing at home so they know where their starting point should be.

Heartbreaks

Buckle your seatbelt, because when we attempt to teach others that our child is capable, we are undoubtedly in for some heartbreaks. Some will always underestimate your child, sometimes grossly. It isn't what we signed up for, but know that you may have to set expectations for others over and over again, even as you teach your child to exercise their own agency and show people themselves what they are capable of.

REFLECT...

- What are caregivers currently doing for your child?

- What personal care, academic, and/or physical tasks does your child legitimately need support and/or accommodations to complete?

- Are there pieces of these tasks that your child may take over, even though your child requires help?

- How can support be systematically decreased over time?

TRY IT ON...

• • • • • • • • • •

- Practice sharing the expectations you have for your child with others. Share your vision of capable with the professionals who work with your child.

- Work with professionals to get goals for phasing out support written into the IEP. How does your child respond? What happens over time to the need for help?

Challenge Your Child (with Support)
in Ways that Regularly Take Them (and You) Outside Your Comfort Zone

GROWING CURIOSITY

Jalen has a love–hate relationship with sound. On the one hand he loves music—everything from Billy Joel and Stevie Wonder to Fatboy Slim. He is so curious that when he hears a new song on his sister's car radio, he immediately records it so he can find it on YouTube later and add it to his playlist. At the same time Jalen hates certain sounds, so much so that he searches for them online as well and plays them over and over so he is prepared when he encounters them in the real world—his own clever kind of DIY desensitization therapy!

His parents only wish this extraordinary curiosity extended to the world around him. Generalized low muscle tone makes walking taxing and a fixed slight bend at his knees makes standing for an extended period uncomfortable. Because of these challenges and a penchant for predictability, Jalen is perfectly content spending his days in his room with his iPod, iPad, and iPhone. His mom Michele says that a consummate "No" is Jalen's first response to most everything he is asked to do. When he was younger, crying and dropping to the floor so characterized Jalen's trips to the grocery store that his mom and dad gave up taking him.

But theirs was a family on the move, and Michele believed Jalen would benefit from traveling, exploring the outdoors, and sharing experiences with his two sisters and brother. Michele was concerned about all of life that Jalen was missing when he was immersed in his techno-driven musical world. Also she could not imagine making family memories without her youngest son.

The goal became getting Jalen to tolerate family trips to amusement parks. Knowing that the amount of walking itself would be daunting, Michele started by having Jalen trek with her to the house next door and back, gradually increasing to two, three, and then four houses until Jalen had conquered the entire block. A membership at LA Fitness and trips to the gym every week was another strategy to up Jalen's endurance.

Once at the amusement park Jalen strongly preferred to sit on a bench with his iPod. Michele laid out the terms of engagement: "Jalen, you get to choose one ride," thinking a single ride would be a good start. No stranger to his mother's resolve, Jalen reluctantly decided upon a ride. Once outside Spaceship Earth at Disney, Jalen threw himself on the ground in the ultimate refusal. Over time, one by one, park by park, Michele increased the expectation that Jalen would choose from one to two, then three, and finally six rides!

Today he takes on almost all rides, including The High Roller, a classic wooden rollercoaster at their local amusement park. His sisters marvel that Jalen always claims the lead seat—the scariest spot on the ride. When the coaster jerks to a stop, they all unload laughing, cheeks flushed from the shared adrenaline rush. They all look to brother Jalen waiting for *him* to pick their next adventure.[1]

The Habit: Capable parents and caregivers challenge their child (with support) in ways that regularly take their child, and likely themselves, outside their comfort zone. These parents recognize that all growth—theirs as well as their children's—is born out of some degree of struggle. Capable parents know that challenges introduced with support are absolutely necessary to move a child to increasing

1   Jalen has Sotos syndrome and autism.

levels of competence. They know that protecting their child from novel or potentially challenging situations may be quicker, more comfortable, less messy, and prettier-looking to outsiders, but that it will ultimately rob their child of the vital experiences they need to grow new skills and competencies.

THE SCIENCE BEHIND THE HABIT

Whether we are talking about an amoeba, a small mammal, or a human, learning and growth emerge from discomfort (Tolle 2008). Pink salmon, nudged out of their comfort zone by rising temperatures, have learned to thrive by migrating out of the Alaskan creeks earlier in the season. Lodgepole pine saplings poke through the ground stretching to seek the energy-generating sun they need to someday frame the mountain skies.

A wise occupational therapist once told me: "Always challenge Jack slightly beyond where he is comfortable, without it he will plateau." She was right.

To be clear, we are not talking about a "thorn in the shoe" or "sleep on a bed of nails" kind of discomfort. In fact, child development experts confirm that adversity during the first three years of life can cause irreparable damage (Felitti *et al.* 1998).

While no child should ever be put in overwhelming or unsupported circumstances, it is a scientific fact that an *appropriate* degree of struggle is the precursor to all new learning. Appropriate struggle is what happens when we leave a toddler with a shape sorter and marvel as they attempt to force the cube into the round hole over and over until at last they drop the square block through the square hole. It is what happens when we encourage that same little one who is clutching our leg at family gatherings to let go and they teeter off to explore the world in toddler-sized bites. Initially scared and unsure they run back again and again, each time going a little further, until finally mastering this challenge and leaving their parents wishing they wouldn't wander so far off.

The power of "safe" challenge

Anyone who has played a video game has felt it. It is the amount of challenge that motivates, encourages, and entices a player to go to a level that is slightly but measurably higher than the one just mastered. This "just right" sweet spot of difficulty, aptly dubbed the "Goldilocks zone" or zone of proximal development (again Vygotsky), accounts for how babies' attention is held by some tasks and not others. In animal learning it is the intuition behind shaping and fading, where dogs are taught complex feats by incrementally increasing the difficulty of a training task.

It is hard to imagine that we could ever rival video games for our child's attention. Homework, household tasks, or even hikes in nature just don't have the built-in bells and whistles of modern virtual worlds. But whether you want to expand your child's horizons or just teach a new skill engaging them *just beyond* their current level is naturally enticing.

Setting the demands too high is sure to frustrate; setting them at status quo may get compliance but will not encourage your child to new levels of performance. Improving my son's core strength would open the door to a host of new skills, including standing, balancing, and walking, which could then lead to lifting toys, kicking balls, ascending stairs, and other activities we all take for granted every day. Lying on his side with his head on the floor was his preferred position for viewing screens—be it the TV or iPad. It was comfortable and did not tax his slack muscles at all. He was content, but was not gaining strength; in fact he was actually losing ground watching shows in that position—muscles atrophying. One ready way to encourage this all-important skill of core strength was to get him to hold his head up in his hands, propped up on his elbows, while lying on his stomach. However, asking him to lie in this position for the length of a cartoon was far too taxing for his slack muscles and he soon collapsed, frustrated and feeling defeated. However, asking him to lie in that position with a book or screen in front of him and increasing the time by one minute increments (about the length of two TikTok videos) enticed him to stay up just a bit longer each time.

We want to intentionally expose our children to what educators call "productive" struggle. Productive struggle describes the effortful learning we engage in when we are faced with problems we don't immediately know how to solve. In the classroom this looks like having students struggle with a word problem where some of the information necessary to solve it is not provided upfront, or when students are asked to build the highest tower they can with straws, paper, clips, and a coin-sized piece of play dough—limiting resources creates a challenge.

Science shows that engaging in such tasks spurs the production of a white substance in the brain called myelin, that increases the strength of brain signals that allow us to get more efficient at doing new things that seem hard at first (Sriram 2020).

Imagine a child's brain as like uncharted pioneer territory. It is hard to traverse. Creating learning through new connections among neurons is like clearing a path and making a dirt road on which to pass. Ultimately we want to turn those dirt roads into paved roads, then freeways, and finally superhighways. At first brain signals can travel, but not quickly or efficiently. But repeated practice—guided by feedback to correct errors—tells the brain that this dirt path isn't good enough. The brain responds by paving the road so that signals can travel faster.

When students first learn a skill, the connections between neurons are weak—like that dirt path. Mastery occurs when those neural connections are built into freeways through the accumulation of myelin allowing information to whiz along unimpeded.

APPLYING THE HABIT

So how can we help our children build freeways in their brains where only dirt paths exist now? The answer in part is by building desirable difficulty (or productive struggle) into daily life. Parents may be thinking, we have more than enough difficulty on our plate, we don't need to purposefully heap on another helping, thank you very much. When my kids were young and I was just trying to get out the door, I became the drill sergeant giving orders: "Get your coat," "Get your backpack." Or else I became Giles the Butler, getting everything lined up for the "little masters" grabbing gym shoes and even putting homework in backpacks. The problem is whether you go drill sergeant or butler, they only get you so far. In the best of circumstances the drill sergeant will get compliance, and the butler will get the job done (because you will do it), but either way your child hasn't learned, grown, or stretched to reach new competencies.

This situation is exacerbated when our kids have disabilities, are neurodivergent, or are task-avoidant. As we discussed in Habit #7, people (including sometimes even us) are always jumping in to do for and supply information when it looks like our child is having difficulty, slower in responding, or just plain needing more processing time. When we are forever supplying information and completing tasks for them, we are denying them the serious brain benefits of productive struggle. Pause and think about building brain highways from dirt paths the next time you stoop to put your child's shoes on, open their snack packaging, or solve their web-based learning questions for them.

Encourage productive struggle at home and with school tasks

Here are three ways to help your child build brain superhighways while just doing life together:

- Ask your child to retrieve information from memory, not just pick it out of a "response lineup."

- Mix up practice instead of always serving it up the same way.

- Space out practice over time.

These may seem like they require a little extra effort at first, but as you build your own neural pathways around "productive struggle" they will become second nature.

Asking your child to retrieve information from memory

You may be surprised to learn that forgetting is a crucial part of learning—it allows us to let go of unimportant stuff to make room for what is critical. Asking kids to retrieve information tells their brain to make more permanent the signals necessary to find that information, and to find it more efficiently next time. If your child is doing homework, a great way to get them to retrieve information is to have them practice answering problems or performing skills before rereading or relearning the material. They will make more mistakes, but they will also learn more. Ask them to recall or "come up with" the correct answer instead of just picking it out. Use songs, motions, and memory devices to teach new things.

With self-care tasks like showering, ask them to show you each step one by one (don't tell them what to do). They may skip the soap-up-the-washcloth step at first, but take heart, they are building brain roads. Or model the steps pretending to shower yourself, leaving one step out. Ask them to show you what you forgot. The act of trying to retrieve steps in the sequence helps the brain build pathways needed to more efficiently find showering information in the future.

Mixing up practice

This may seem counterproductive at first—why not just get one thing down before starting another? But mixing up practice on new tasks causes struggle that tells the brain to construct better roads.

Whenever possible, challenge your child to use their long-term memory instead of solely relying on what was just learned, said, or taught. Instead of having your child complete the same after-dinner chore they are comfortable with over and over, switch it up. After you have initially taught them two skills like drying dishes and loading the dishwasher, alternate the days that you ask them to do each. Depending on your child's skill level, divide the job into mini tasks and mix up practice between these—like alternating loading silverware one day and loading plates the next. It is important that you work at a level that challenges just beyond where your child is currently comfortable. If it is not too frustrating, add a third task to the rotation. Your child will initially make more mistakes, and you have to be okay with that; but remember, these mistakes are "productive" because they are building better roads.

Spacing out practice over time

Spreading practice evenly over time is one of the most helpful techniques for deepening learning. Our brains benefit from frequent shorter practice sessions as opposed to less frequent long ones. Research with students shows that those who space out their learning outperform students who try to learn in longer sessions, even if those who spaced out their learning spent less total time on task.

Parents, this one is in our wheelhouse. You are probably already spacing out practice over time with your child without even recognizing it. Whenever you have your child practice a hygiene task like bathing, teeth brushing, toileting, or hand washing every day over time, or do a regular chore like taking out the garbage, mowing grass, or making a bed, you are helping them build brain power. If you are doing a version of any of the above, give yourself points for this one! Remember too that these practice sessions don't have to be long. Short practice opportunities offered consistently over time are best for building neural pathways. This can work well for our children who struggle with attention or who have sensory issues. For example, it is just as effective from a brain learning perspective to have your child take two short showers a day, instead of requiring them to complete all shower steps at once. Don't be concerned if the practice is short, the key is just keep repeating it over time to build the skill.

Learning is not about turning on a light. Instead, it's about constructing better and faster roads. Smart brains are efficient brains, and that efficiency comes from myelinating brain wires through repeated practice with specific feedback.

Signs the struggle has become unproductive

Offering other options, modeling (e.g., see how I brush each tooth in small circles), and verbal praise or other signs of encouragement can keep a challenge productive. But when does an otherwise productive struggle become unproductive? If there are obvious signs that your child is getting frustrated or dysregulated, offer a new "helpful" piece of information or make it a game to help your child get started. If a child feels rushed, or the time he needs to adequately process a task is annoying or getting in others' way, or they are missing out on something more fun, they will likely disengage, so pick the times you challenge your child carefully. When he becomes visibly frustrated, learning has likely stopped. The best course of action is to take a break and try again later.

The struggle is real

Okay, point made! Moving slightly beyond our comfort zone (with support) is a sure-fire way to encourage growth, and the appropriate amount of struggle is food for growing brains. But parenting, particularly parenting a child with a disability, is a study in struggle all its own. There are lots of legitimate reasons we don't challenge our kids. It is work, it requires intentionality and commitment, and oftentimes we are righteously exhausted.

Take heart, introducing productive struggle doesn't have to be difficult for you. Use the simple checklist below to see how you are doing at challenging your child with support. If you are trying these things, you are doing your part to productively challenge your child, encourage growth, and avoid skill atrophy. It may feel harder than just giving kids the answer or doing things for them, but a simple cost–benefit analysis says it all:

Time spent letting your child try on their own before helping: Seconds. Seeing your child's smile when they know they have done it themselves: Priceless!

Some discomfort yes, but these are returns that last a lifetime!

STRUGGLE WITH SUPPORT CHECKLIST

☐ I wait before jumping in with a solution, to allow my child to grapple with questions, manipulate materials, and process information to formulate their own response.

☐ I introduce new tasks, challenges, and responsibilities in short meaningful bites.

☐ I alternate the skills I ask my child to practice.

☐ I challenge my child to supply, find, or show me answers or steps in a sequence, rather than only having them pick out information.

☐ I am aware where my child is opting out of activities, tasks, and experiences and search for ways to help them opt in.

There is still plenty of room for comfort

It is true that children learn from challenges. Some struggle builds neural pathways and increases efficiency over time. Just like Goldilocks with her chair, porridge, and bed, the "just right" amount of struggle feels good to our brains even when it starts out a little uncomfortable. But every rule has its exceptions. There are times and conditions when struggle does not feel good and should not be attempted. You know your child best. It goes without saying that challenge only works when our child feels loved and supported. There are other legitimate circumstances in which to reduce demands, like when your child is dysregulated or when their nervous system is overtaxed. Other conditions, such as autistic burnout, call for reduced demands, alongside support and "gentle" encouragement for your child.

When safer, more comfortable, and easier isn't "all that"

For Jack and me it all went back to that day at the New Jersey shore when a trip to the beach seemed too taxing. "Wouldn't he be safer, more comfortable, and more content at home?" This question crossed my mind not only that sunny morning but literally hundreds of other times during Jack's growing up. My answer each time was "Maybe so." Jack would be safer if he was not allowed to dangle unceremoniously from a zipline, or straddle second floor banisters. Certainly, he would be more comfortable if allowed to lie on his side in front of the TV, or if pecking at computer keys instead of grasping a pencil. He would definitely be more content with all his favorite toys and books within arm's reach. If not much was asked of Jack, life looked pretty, there was no protest or struggle. And who didn't love happy Jack with his contagious smile? But there was also no growth, no clapping for surprise milestones met, and little cause for pride in new accomplishments.

I had made my mind up back at the shore, I did not want easy, safe, or comfortable for Jack, because with that would come complacency and boredom—one big flat plateau. One parent I work with calls it "leaning into the challenge." Whenever she sees her child struggling with or wanting to opt out of something she believes is possible for her, she encourages her daughter to hang in there and try again. When I think of my own son, I am reminded of that classic board game, Candyland. I realized that for my kid, choosing the red and white ribbon-shaped slide marked "easy route", while fun in the moment, would come at the expense of gaining skills, competencies, and the sense of accomplishment that accompanies learning something new.

I worried that too much "opting out" would leave an indelible mark that over time would result in my child coming to believe that he was not capable.

I could not risk letting Jack internalize that he was "less than." I concluded that it was not only okay to be less comfortable, less safe, it was quite possibly more desirable and, in fact, therapeutic. Jack had a syndrome. If I wanted him to escape the limitations that accompanied that diagnosis, I felt I could not afford to play it "safe." I saw successive challenges posed with support as the way out for my kid.

There is dignity in taking risks and grappling with challenges. I wanted to keep all options open for Jack. Even if it was painful, inconvenient, more embarrassing, or took more time.

If we allowed him to opt out this time, it would be even easier to opt out the next time and the next, until a pattern was established. This was a pattern that had the potential to impact him for a lifetime. Therefore, as counterintuitive as it sounds, I vigorously pursued (the "just right" amount of) discomfort for my son.

Making sure that security blankets don't become barriers to growth

Capable parents are always on the lookout for how to help their child to grow in their skills and be prepared to take on new responsibilities over time. One place to look is areas where your child has been allowed to opt out or where they have been exempted or excluded in the past.

For many children with challenges, screen time, food, or a familiar toy or activity provide comfort and can serve as security blankets. The problem arises when they become a substitute for challenge or exploring their world.

There is not a parent on the planet that has not used the TV or iPad as a babysitter, but for my son, I feared it could become a surrogate for living life.

Think about the challenges, great and small, that your child faces on a daily basis. Now think about these challenges given your vision of capable you have with your child. Where you choose comfort and where you choose challenge depends on your shared vision. Ask yourself the following questions about the role of challenge in your child's life, remembering that with the "just right amount of challenge" every child may explore outside their comfort zone.

REFLECT...

- Are there tasks or activities that you are allowing your child to opt out of?

- Are there things you are fearful about your child doing/trying/ being?

- What are you doing that teaches your child to welcome "challenge" in their life?

- What are ways you could support your child to approach challenging tasks or situations instead of avoiding them?

- What does your child turn to for comfort and security?

- How do these things serve you and/or your relationship with your child?

- To what extent have these devices, activities, foods, or things become a substitute for challenge and exploration?

TRY IT ON...

- Use a journal or your phone to reflect on where you are prioritizing comfort over challenge for your child. Think about why you are choosing comfort. Identify one specific area where your child would benefit from challenge. What would it take to engage your child in productive struggle in that area? Could you use any of the three strategies above to help your child build new neural pathways?

- Define the trade-offs for your child and yourself of choosing comfort over challenge in one specific area. Revisit your shared vision of capable and the role of challenge in meeting the vision.

- Identify one comfort activity, food, or device. Explore how you can encourage your child to tolerate time away from that comfort. What opportunities and what difficulties does that challenge create? Can you increase the time that your child engages in desired activities and behaviors?

- Identify an area, or areas, in which you see your child plateauing or stalling in their development. Make a plan for supporting him in stepping out and expanding in that area.

Walk Alongside Professionals
to Help Your Child Learn How They Learn Best and Get Them the Support and Services They Need

ACCORDING TO THE BOOK OF QUINN

Quinn felt like a human ping-pong ball. The only thing that was predictable was that he would be bounced from the life skills class to the general education class and back to life skills again. On any given day, for about 30 minutes, you would find him at a desk alongside other children with hands raised, answering questions after story time. Later Quinn could be seen fidgeting on the carpet in life skills class, watching and waiting, as the teacher was practicing the *b* sound with one child, while another was banging a wooden wagon into overstuffed toy shelves delighting in the thunderous noise it made. Jackie knew that the chaos was getting to Quinn when he began imitating noises he heard other students making and melting down in the after-school pickup line.

Educationally speaking, Quinn was a puzzle not easily solved. Jackie lamented that if it took each teacher three months to figure out her son, he would lose roughly a semester each school year. Doing the math, she concluded that Quinn did not have the luxury of time to waste. Life skills were important, no doubt, but Jackie was convinced that he could also learn academics alongside general education students.

Jackie was fond of telling teachers, "You have to 'learn' my kid before you can teach him. Give Quinn a concrete reason to learn, visual models, lots of repetition, and limit his answer choices, and that kid can catch on to almost anything."

When it came time to master state capitals in fourth-grade geography, teachers informed Jackie that they were going to teach him only a select few northern and southern states. Jackie felt that learning random states would prove confusing and out of context for Quinn. She told the teacher that he could learn them all. "Teach a few capitals at a time, adding a few more in as you go. Teach them different ways with maps, puzzles, computer games. And when you quiz him, give him a word bank. Later you can ask him to give them back to you cold." A month and a half later the teacher caught Jackie in the hallway, she was beaming. Quinn had performed better on the final test than many of his "typical" classmates.

Geographic knowledge of the states and their capitals proved to be more than just obscure "factoids" for Quinn. As the years passed, he retained this information and used it in real life to do things like understand the distance between where he lived in rural Missouri and where a tornado had just touched down, and how far his relatives from other states had to travel to visit him.

The sixth-grade teacher, Ms. Renner, started out incredulous but was an enthusiastic convert when she saw how Quinn could grasp content when given context, visuals, repetition, and clear response choices. Ms. Renner immortalized Jackie's counsel about how Quinn learns best in a book dedicated just to him. This binder that came to be known as the "Book of Quinn" was reliably passed on from teacher to teacher and grade to grade until it was lost, an unfortunate casuality of the transition from middle school to high school.

Nevertheless, Jackie went on sharing wisdom from the Book of Quinn. The knowledge within helped teachers set Quinn up for learning everything from earth science to Spanish alongside high school friends.

This year Quinn proudly strutted the entire distance of the stage to shake the hand of the principal and receive his modified high school diploma. Although Quinn's post-school future is still a mystery, you can be sure that Quinn and his mom will continue to pass on lessons from the Book of Quinn to the professionals who work with him.[1]

The Habit: Capable parents keep two things in mind as they make decisions for and with their child. They recognize that while the caring professionals who work with their child are experts in their fields, they are experts in their child. As the people who know their child best, they share their knowledge of how their child best (1) learns, (2) communicates, and (3) relates to others to get their child what they need. They partner with professionals, coupling their knowledge and insight with the teachers', therapists', and doctors' expertise to maximize their child's potential. While acknowledging professional expertise, they keep their vision of capable (Habit #3) front and center and use it to judge the desirability of the supports, services, accommodations, and modifications that are offered to their child. All the while they help their child build precious self-knowledge so that their child can take advantage of their own learning opportunities and advocate for the supports and services that help them thrive.

THE SCIENCE BEHIND THE HABIT

Kids are constantly growing, learning, and changing before our very eyes. It is no secret that children are sponges drinking in through their senses all they see and hear their parents doing. Studies show this begins even in the womb, as unborn infants sense and take on their mother's mood and stress levels. The body of research on emotional coregulation proves that parents and children are constantly taking in data from one another, essentially "learning" each other.

Parents are their child's first and most impactful teachers. One only needs elementary math to see how this works out. Unless your

1   Quinn has Down syndrome and Type 1 diabetes.

child lives in a residential school, even the best teachers and other support professionals only "have" your child for about five and a half hours a day maximum. Your child is with you (or the caregiver you designate) the approximately 18 or so hours a day that they are not with these other folk! It stands to reason that you know your child better than anyone, and as such you are in the best position to observe your child and make informed decisions with (and about) your child regarding their growth and learning.

Although we parents have the natural bond with and spend the most time with our child, we are in no way expected to do it all. "Thank God!" you think. Learning, communication, and behavior needs are more complex for kids with disabilities than for their "neurotypical" peers. In the United States in 1973 US Federal Education law formally recognized that children with disabilities and who are neurodivergent benefit the most from a coordinated team approach that considers the needs of the whole child. This is the genesis of the Individualized Education Plan (IEP) team. Other developed countries employ a similar team approach.

APPLYING THE HABIT

Walking alongside professionals

To understand this notion of "walking alongside" I borrow with gratitude from an anonymous but often-quoted African proverb. It goes like this: "If you want to go fast, go alone; but if you want to go far, go together." Wise counsel for parents seeking the greatest measure of benefit for their child.

I have seen versions of these prophetic words play out again and again over the past 30 years with countless families and in my own life as well. Those of us who go too fast and too hard often burn bridges with the professionals who have the knowledge, skills, resources, and on-the-ground insights to help their child. If we go this route we often burn out as well, souring on the systems and supports designed to help our child. If our very understandable, and sometimes desperate, attempts to secure what we believe our child needs are not satisfied on our timeline, we feel we must make our demands harder and louder. If we perceive that our child's needs are being ignored or passed over, too many of us adopt a victim mentality. This mindset and the dysregulated nervous systems it fosters does nothing to help our child and may even hurt our child as he or she absorbs our negative energy.

Whether your child is neurodivergent or neurotypical you learn pretty quickly (somewhere between that first sleepless night and signing up for preschool) that you're in for a marathon and not a sprint. That gets us back to the second part of the proverb, "if you want to go far, go together." Raising your child to be capable doesn't happen overnight or as the result of one "magical" classroom, behavior aide, therapist, or state-of-the-art technology tool. It *is* the result of scores of microdecisions made over time using a combination of expertise, intentionality, intuition, and data about how your child learns best. It requires dogged consistency, patience, follow-through, personal connection, and, yes, love, delivered on time every day. Neither parents nor professionals can fly solo. Even homeschool parents draw support from published curricula, therapists, and content specialists.

Just like you need them, the professionals need you. They can't produce a capable kid on their own. Given burgeoning caseloads across disciplines, teachers, therapists, and doctors don't have the time, and they require the precious expertise in your child that only you possess. It is only through collaboration that your child gets down the long road to becoming capable. To go far you'll need a team.

With the exception of a very narrow slice of disgruntled, misplaced souls, most who enter the fields of education, therapy, cognitive science, and medicine do so because they want to use all the tools and skills in their power to positively impact the lives of the children they serve. At the same time the policies and structures of the institutions in which these dedicated professionals work can be slow, stubborn, and outdated, at times appearing painfully tone deaf to the very real needs of children. Even the most caring professionals when indoctrinated in flawed educational or medical models can appear out of step with the needs of the children they are employed to reach. A case manager believes Sam's behavioral needs require a 1:1 aide, but school policies only allow for aides for children with certain diagnoses or in specific cases; a teacher wants to challenge a twice exceptional child in ways that she thinks will authentically engage him, but large class sizes make it nearly impossible; an occupational therapist recommends an assistive device to enhance communication, but there are no funds available to pay for it; ...the list goes on and on.

"Walking alongside" means we clearly communicate what we believe our child needs to achieve their vision of capable, and we collaborate with professionals to ensure that those needs are met.

It presumes no hierarchy. It is neither parents demanding services nor professionals dictating limitations. Nor is it parents holding their tongues and accepting substandard support or services that are mismatched to their child's needs because that is just "what is available." Walking alongside is active, not passive.

Rather than getting tangled up in adversarial relationships, capable parents recognize that each of the teachers, therapists, aides, and doctors who are part of their child's learning journey offers something unique. Each of them holds expertise that addresses a facet of human development that is critical to your child's success. But even as they possess unique competence in their chosen fields, capable parents never forget that they know better than anyone not only their child's challenges but also their unique gifts, interests, and heart's desires.

Successful teams that will take your child "far" require attention, communication, creativity, and cooperation. Parents who partner with professionals to get their child what they need agree on the "what" (desired outcome) and are creative in terms of the "how" (strategies to get there). If your child has an IEP, follow the six steps of the "partnering with professionals" process below to ensure that your child's plan is aligned with your shared vision of capable.

1. *Observe your child's learning and behavior.* Pay attention to how they learn and behave at different times of the day and in different settings (e.g., bedtime, parties with lots of stimuli,

during homework). Identify the situations, times of day, and people that are challenging and comforting for your child.

2. *Talk with your child about what works for them.* Ask questions and communicate with your child about what feels good to them when they are learning, what helps them focus, and what makes them want to work harder and spend time with others.

3. *Clearly communicate the vision of capable to the team.* Share with the team the vision of capable you hold with your child (see Habit #3) as well as the support and services you believe your child needs to reach that vision.

4. *Agree on the desired outcome with the team (the what).* Come to agreement with the IEP team on what the desired outcome of services is. Ensure that it is written into the relevant section of the IEP.

5. *Consider alternatives for meeting the desired outcome (the how).* Listen to the team, restate possible concerns to make sure you understand them, and be open to creative ways to meet the desired outcome.

6. *Agree on a plan to meet desired outcomes.* Agree on a plan and a schedule for review. Be prepared to revise the plan as necessary—the "how" can vary as long as it does not compromise the "what."

LEO, HIS DAD, AND AMERICAN HISTORY

Leo has moved to a new high school in a new district and he and his dad are meeting with the IEP team to determine services.

1. *Observe your child's learning and behavior.*

   Leo's dad notes that at home he and his wife need to read big chunks of homework assignments to Leo. They have seen him rely on the support of teaching assistants to participate in World History and American History classes in his previous school district.

2. *Talk with your child about what works for them.*

   Leo's dad talks to him about his classes. Leo says he gets anxious when the teacher assigns longer reading assignments and that he falls behind when the teacher gives in-class time to read. He is not always sure of how or when to use technology tools to help get his answers down.

3. *Clearly communicate the vision of capable to the team.*

   Leo and his dad share with the team that their vision is that Leo complete all the high school coursework leading to a modified diploma.

4. *Agree on the desired outcome with the team (the what).*

   Leo, his dad, and the team agree that the desired outcome is for Leo to work toward the curriculum standards necessary to complete American History as required for a modified diploma.

5. *Consider alternatives for meeting the desired outcome (the how).*

   Leo and his dad: Based on his performance in previous "print heavy" classes at his last high school, Leo needs a consistent 1:1 aide to help with reading assignments, read questions, and scribe answers for him to work toward American History standards.

   IEP team: We believe that a consistent 1:1 aide will ultimately be too confining for Leo as he moves toward graduation. We propose providing an aide for four to six weeks during American History class, phasing out to Leo using a combination of the Natural Reader app to read text and Speech-to-Text in Google Docs to scribe his responses.

6. *Agree on a plan to meet desired outcomes.*

Leo and his dad: That solution can work as long as we agree to weekly check-ins between Leo and his special education case manager. If they determine that the quality of his understanding of the content is suffering, the 1:1 aide resumes for four weeks during American History class and the school provides time outside of class to offer Leo additional training and support in using Natural Reader and Speech-to-Text technology tools. After that we can begin trying again to phase out aide support.

Communicate how your child learns best

Let teachers/clinicians know how your child learns best. Offer specific examples whenever you can. Remember that they have expertise in their field but you are the expert in your child.

Communicate strengths that you see, including non-school ones (e.g., my child loves to draw comics, he loves to write, she will light up if you play "You Are My Sunshine," squishy feeling objects always get his attention, a cool room activates her muscle tone, etc.). Consider all strengths and interests so that school personnel can leverage them to support challenges.

Self-understanding is the key

Getting our children what they need to succeed starts with helping *them* get in touch with how they learn. We parents observe, and over time, with the help of teachers, therapists, and doctors, we gain useful insights about how and under what conditions our child best learns, communicates, and relates. But our possessing these insights is not enough; this knowledge and awareness needs to reside within your child. Helping your child get in touch with how they learn reminds me of the law-enforcement campaign "If you see something, say something." With urgent concerns ruling the day we often don't take time to pause and talk with our child about how they learn and how they are feeling about their learning. "Saying something" can take the form of statements or questions:

- *Call it out.* Make a point of calling out what we see happening with our child. When we notice our child learning, communicating, or relating well, and we let them know, we are helping them build priceless self-knowledge in the form of new understandings about how they best absorb new information, express their creativity, calm and regulate their nervous system, and/or relate to others.

- *Ask questions.* Thoughtful questions can turn our child's attention to how they are feeling in the moment. Ask about their experience. "Did you feel like you were able to focus on the story better while wearing the weighted blanket?" "Was it easier to get your ideas out after jotting down notes?" "Did making a mental picture or seeing a social story help you get along with the kids in after-school care?"

If our child does not respond, that is okay, they might not know how they feel. We return to the first strategy of calling out what we see. We continue to make observations based on what we see and notice in our child. This borrows from a sensory technique called "declarative language" that uses statements to help kids tune in and internalize what they are feeling. Statements like "I notice that you get to your calm place quicker when you sit in the bean bag chair," "It looks like you are accurate with math problems when you wear the noise canceling headphones," or "You know, when you were checking your picture schedule you did not miss a single step in showering."

Because we parents are with our child so much we are in a unique position to help them build priceless self-knowledge about their learning preferences and encourage habits that not only make learning stick, but make it more fun as well.

When school gets in the way of learning

Sadly, what sounds like an oxymoron is actually true. School can get in the way of learning. As I have said many times and in many ways throughout these pages, kids are wired to learn. However, for many neurotypical and neurodivergent kids, how we "do school" discourages them from applying their biological wiring to school tasks. Rigid curricula, achievement testing, judgments of others, and social pressure can squelch kids' curiosity toward all things academic. This unfortunate reality has given way to a robust movement aptly called "Unschooling," which is fueled by kids' natural curiosity and innate desire to learn. Unschooling takes off the pressure for traditional "achievement," builds on kids' interests, and promotes self-knowledge and advocacy.

This is not feel-good educational fluff for an entitled generation. Unschooling is rooted in sound ideas that make intuitive sense— ideas that should be built into all learning settings, inside and outside schools. We all want our children to be motivated, self-directed lifelong learners. But getting there can be complicated for high-need students who require more structure, support, accommodations, and modifications in order to thrive, or for students who have experienced trauma brought on by the very same school experiences that were intended to help them learn in the first place.

Too risky to learn

We parents have to partner with school staff to help kids take risks that ignite learning. Like so many kids who have experienced school trauma, by the time he was in middle school my son approached studying defensively. Like a boxer in the ring bobs and weaves to protect a cracked rib from further injury, he worked hard to shield anything that he did not know from prying eyes. He practiced facts he already knew over and over and refused to study or quiz himself on what he did not know. All of this, an elaborate dance to avoid the all-too-familiar feelings of failure brought on by a cruel hodgepodge of arenas where he had not "measured up" in the past. He was not about to make himself vulnerable again by taking on academic risks—and who would blame him!

However, we know that all learning requires some degree of risk. We are more likely to take chances and step out of our comfort zone when we feel safe. So then, how do we encourage curiosity and academic adventurism when our kids have more complicated needs and every reason to want to avoid taking academic risks?

Identify and leverage special interests

Unfortunately grades, tests, and peer pressure shine a flashing neon spotlight on "weaknesses." We parents, the most influential people in our child's life, need to be on the lookout for our child's natural interests and always mine for strengths. Trust what you see in your child over the proclamations of her label or diagnosis. Don't be too reliant on a diagnosis that boils your child down to an oversimplified set of characteristics. Look for where they defy their diagnosis. For example, ADHD may mark your child as not able to remain on task, but you notice that she can focus for hours when the topic is women's rights, environmental sustainability, the history of soccer, or cryptocurrency.

Clearly communicate your child's special interests to their teachers and therapists and encourage your child to communicate these as well. Ask teachers to incorporate your child's interests into assignments to increase motivation and buy-in. The majority of teachers welcome any hook that will increase student engagement—in the end, heightened engagement makes their job easier and more rewarding. Even if your child's interests or strengths don't exactly map onto a particular school task you may be able to use them to build momentum for a school task. Suggest learning to calculate area by measuring the soccer field, learning science by retrieving water samples from the nearby lake and testing them, learning how to develop a three-paragraph essay via a persuasive campaign promoting women's health, or learning to debate through a matchup of crypto vs. traditional currency.

Of course, you and the professionals who work with your child need to keep specific challenges and weaknesses front-of-mind, but give at least equal effort to identifying your child's unique assets, motivations, and predilections. Do not ignore these interests as they may give him or her an edge in overcoming academic challenges.

Identify and leverage specific learning strengths

In addition to special interests, look too at the specific learning skills and processes which are at the root of our children's struggle. Here again find possibilities—the subskills and pieces of the learning process that your child is good at—and call them out. "You struggle remembering facts, but you love reading! Since you are a good reader you can always reread to recall facts," "You see things so well in pictures, you can use that ability to draw models to help you with division and with geometry," "You thrive when the rules are clear and consistent, you can use that ability to help you plug in the numbers and feel confident that you will get the correct answer every time as long as you stick to the formula," "You love music, we can create songs together so that you don't forget the rules at school." In this way you use strengths, even "micro" ones, to help to build the confidence and safety needed to get our kids to venture into learning.

Most parents are not educational or developmental psychology gurus, nor should we have to be. Find a trusted teacher or therapist and pick their brain to tease out the nuances behind the labels and generalized terminology that has been applied to your child such as "developmentally delayed," "on the spectrum," "learning disabled," "cognitive processing delay," "sensory disorder," and "intellectually impaired." Take the term "sensory processing disorder." The same label is used to describe severe sensory-seeking behavior and severe sensory avoidance behavior. Where do these terms ring true in describing your child's learning, behavior, and communication patterns and where do they fall short?

Keep in mind that while a label seeks to sort and simplify, your child is an individual that defies categorization. The specific uniquenesses that make your child who he is may help him defy the odds laid down by his diagnosis.

Hats off to teaching heroes

Kids have a sixth sense for detecting whether or not their teachers believe in them, and they mirror those expectations. In our case, those teachers were the ones who truly "saw" my kid and offered support, without any "woe is you, poor kid" hint of compromise in their voices. These everyday heroes were not concerned with just "checking the boxes" and then giving insincere grades to the "special" kid. They went the extra mile to engage him and enticed him to try again, and try harder when that didn't work. They did not "do for" my kid just to expedite getting the task at hand done. They offered support, but only after they gave him a wide berth to respond on his own. They honored him with the ultimate dignity of holding him accountable when he performed below what they knew he could do. When my teenage son thought he could mask his fear of failure with old-fashioned disrespectful behavior that featured laying his head on the desk and a mumbled "I don't care" retort to virtually every attempt to engage, one of these teaching heroes calmly responded, "Not caring does not let you off the hook for learning in my class, so tell me what you do care about."

Whether general or special education, there are those teachers who simply operate from a "success" default. They flat out believe the best of each of their students and continually challenge them to do their best. Make friends with and learn from these gifted individuals. Acknowledge, encourage, and leverage their positive energy to help your child thrive.

Getting smart about using therapies to get to "capable"

Our children often require more than the standard educational fare to reach their potential. It is not unusual for a child who has a disability or who is neurodivergent to work with four or five different therapists in the course of a week. Occupational, physical, speech, behavioral, and sensory are among the traditional therapies, but beyond the "standard" therapies, parents are met with innumerable additional therapy possibilities, all which claim to help their child overcome specific deficits, relieve anxiety, increase neuroplasticity, and build skills. These include neurofeedback, vitamin megadosing, and cranial sacral, music, art, and hyperbaric oxygen therapy, just to name a few.

Unless the therapy is built into the school day, your child is spending valuable time transitioning to and from appointments. Be intentional and consider the purpose that each serves in light of your vision of capable for your child. Just because a technique is trending does not mean that it will help your child meet your shared vision.

Devising DIY therapy

The right therapy or combination of therapies can be game-changing for your child. But maximum benefit is rarely achieved solely through scheduled appointments. When compared to neurotypical peers, most children with disabilities need exponentially more practice to gain skills and to catch up on missed developmental building blocks. Assuming your child is going to overcome developmental delays in scheduled therapy sessions alone is akin to a person seeking to lose weight by only counting points assigned to the foods they eat during their hour-long WeightWatchers group meetings.

We parents can multiply the benefits of therapy by supplementing at home with "do-it-yourself" DIY therapy exercises. These are self-styled practice opportunities that address the goals identified by your speech, occupational, physical, or behavioral therapist. Because DIY therapy takes advantage of regularly occurring opportunities as they present themselves throughout the day, there is no end to the practice possibilities they generate.

Calculate the time your child spends in therapy. This is precious time with a skilled professional, but once you take out travel time to and from the therapist's office, you may find that the total time your child is working on necessary skills and deficits is woefully short.

"CRUSHING IT"—WITH GARLIC

If Jack relied solely on the programmed opportunities offered by his therapists, I feared he would always remain behind—struggling through or not completing simple tasks that his peers took for granted, like lifting himself out of a pool, blowing out birthday candles, grasping a pencil, or finishing a meal in a timely fashion. By my calculations the time between scheduled appointments was at least as important as the time in them. Every time we pulled into our driveway after our nearly two-hour travel time to and from occupational therapy, physical therapy, or speech therapy, I was reminded of the fact that the time Jack spent sitting strapped in a booster seat was longer than his actual "therapeutic minutes."

Of course, all of these skilled therapists encouraged practice between sessions and, consistent with their recommendations, we were working at home. Still, for me the tick of the opportunity clock was deafening. I was dogged by a nagging sense that I had to do more to find and leverage that precious "time between" scheduled sessions. I scanned our day for preferred and necessary tasks that would automatically work the multitude of small muscles that Jack needed to strengthen. I turned to a mix of feigned and real requests for meal prep help to create practice opportunities to build strength, balance, endurance, and confidence in my young son.

Every time a jar or can needed to be opened in our house (and often even when one didn't) I matter-of-factly sat it in front of Jack saying I needed help from my strong boy. He would battle with the jar or can opener, but because it seemed like I assumed he could do these things and because they needed to get done for dinner to materialize, he did them.

Garlic crushing turned out to be a most convenient source of hand strengthening. Although my Midwest German heritage has its own culinary traditions, my husband's family influence won out where meals were concerned. His father was the son of Sicilian immigrants, and his mother schooled me in delicious Italian specialties like pasta with broccoli and anchovy, ricotta-stuffed shells, and spaghetti sauce Sicilian style with short ribs and hard-boiled eggs. Each of these requires a generous portion of garlic. If Jack was not in the kitchen, I would save the task and call him down from his room for the express purpose of squeezing the garlic crusher—a job which drew together all of the small muscles in the center of his palm. I often overstated the number of cloves needed, which multiplied the practice. As a result, our family consumed an abundance of garlic and Jack got in a lot of repeat practice. He became my official garlic crusher, and today, as an adult, he continues to have that domestic distinction in our home.

We found and took full advantage of these and other regularly occurring DIY therapies including weight-bearing with full grocery bags, core-strengthening with banister workouts, and tongue-lifting with peanut butter dollops. Each of these in their own way served to accelerate progress toward formal therapy goals.

Meal prep turned out to be our go-to for devising strengthening exercises because it was natural and convenient for us. Consider your context. What regularly occurring opportunities exist in your child's world? Maybe you can take advantage of your family farm, landscaping business, or hair salon, or use your geographic location near water or in nature as a source of therapy practice. The possibilities are endless. But whatever you choose, be intentional and consistent. Your goal is getting in as many repetitions as possible without making it feel like "practice" to your child.

Replacing or augmenting therapy over time

Devising "DIY therapy" does not mean dismissing therapy and going it on your own. Home-grown exercises are meant to exponentially increase progress and are actually a way to walk alongside trained professionals in meeting your child's therapy goals. Discontinuing therapy, canceling counseling sessions, or pretending that services are not necessary does not make your child capable, and refusing services does not magically dissolve your child's deficits.

However, it is true that the usefulness of various therapies is bound to change over your child's lifespan. Be intentional about determining if and when your child has met the break-even point with a particular service. I define the break-even point as the point where your child has reaped all the benefits that a particular therapy has to offer. Depending on the child this point may be influenced by a number of things, including the extent to which therapy can mimic functional, meaningful skills, the availability of other community activities that meet therapy goals, and the messages the child may be taking away from receiving multiple therapies over extended periods of time.

As your child matures, be on the lookout for signs that a therapy has come to feel contrived for them and identify ways to replace it with community activities that address the same goals and provide the meaningful practice (gym memberships, run clubs, martial arts, dance classes, art classes, or recreational sports, etc.).

Taking advantage of regularly occurring activities that exist in your community to practice skills not only supercharges therapy, they can actually ignite genuine interests. In this way your child can maintain gains made in a whole host of areas including strength, balance, muscle control, motor-planning coordination, endurance, speech, and confidence, while at the same time developing a lifelong pursuit. My son traded physical therapy for personal training and cross-country running. Other kids have found personal satisfaction and growth through tae kwon do, dance, art studio time, yoga, Dungeons & Dragons, and recreational sports.

More is [not] always better

As with all things, your vision of capable becomes the litmus test for the therapies, support, and supplemental services your child is offered. If your child is evaluated and receives a label through the education system, they become eligible for a suite of services, supports, and accommodations associated with the educational label.

But just because a service or support is offered, it does not necessarily follow that you have to accept it. Again, you are the expert in your child, but it can be nearly impossible to determine which supports to accept and which to pass on. Sometimes we are so hungry for our child's needs to be addressed that we jump at services. Or sometimes the barrage of choices surrounding services is so confounding that the path of least resistance is just to say yes to them all. The conventional wisdom is that more is better, right? In some cases yes, but not necessarily. The case managers, therapists, and special educators who work with your child have invaluable knowledge. Take their counsel, but remember you know your child best. Look carefully at the trade-offs.

If I sleep in I get a few extra ZZZ. That is good, but I miss my workout. The same is true with supplemental services and therapies. There are trade-offs and opportunity costs for your child. I accept the literacy time in the hallway, and my son misses time interacting with peers in the social studies class. Driving my child to a friend's club for social skills development provides direct social skills training, but causes them to miss making connections and getting comfortable with neighborhood kids.

There are instances where the need for therapy is obvious and worth any trade-off, these are the easy choices. However, sometimes the choices are not so obvious. When these dilemmas present themselves, return to the vision of capable you have built with your child. Consider therapies, supports, and supplemental services in light of the competencies the vision imagines.

Services should flow from goals, not labels or diagnoses.

Ask yourself, does the proposed service address a specific skill in which my son or daughter displays a deficit? Do I have reason to believe that this service will make my child more independent, mentally or physically agile, verbal, or tolerant? If not, you may politely decline the service and free up that time for another service, activity, or experience that will enhance your child's quality of life, increase his access to the community, or build essential skills.

There can be extraordinary circumstances, additional variables, and special opportunities that you want to capture for your child. For instance, another child may be receiving a service at the same time as your child, and you determine the opportunity for an organic friendship makes investing time in that service worth it. Take heart, there is only so much you can know, and you will make mistakes. The best guide remains your shared vision of capable. Armed with the vision and informed by your child's interests and passion, trust your gut.

PULLING OUT—WHEN SUPPORT CLASHES WITH YOUR GOALS

Literally bumping into my son in the hallway at school created a degree of cognitive dissidence that I needed to reconcile. I was volunteering for the school book fair and he was sitting at a little desk with an instructional aide practicing what I was told was pre-reading and number sense. Upon further inquiry I learned Jack was receiving this support two to three times a week. At first blush, I thought, what's not to like? What primary-aged student could not benefit from a double dose of letters and numbers? His twin sister could have even benefited from this. Only she couldn't because she did not have Jack's label. It turned out, this service was an extra benefit doled out to all students with my son's special education distinction. Don't look a gift-horse in the mouth, right? Here lies the exception to this widely accepted piece of pop-wisdom. When I stared down this horse, I did not like what I saw.

Digging further I learned that this extra support came at the expense of social studies class time. Two to three days a week he was missing the first-grade version of studying people and places with his classmates. This is where the dissidence lived— somewhere between this perfectly reasonable support and my goal for my kid. I envisioned Jack connecting with other kids and moving through the elementary grades as a full member of his class. Given our vision, this "pull out" service thwarted the end game. It set Jack apart from his peers, and in that way it was, in fact, no gift at all. I politely declined the service and requested an IEP amendment to make my request official.

In Jack's case, this was a "generic" support attached to his label. Our kids are not homogeneous—some kids bearing his label may have needed reading and math support in the hall, but our vision dictated that Jack needed interaction with same-aged peers more. The fact is children's services should flow from goals, not labels or diagnoses.

Depending on the school district, various diagnoses and labels carry with them a broad range of services. Ensure that each specialized service written into your child's IEP is there for one purpose—and that is to build the skills and competencies necessary to achieve their specific goals consistent with your vision. If you can't figure out how a support is supporting your shared vision for your child, it probably should not be there. Ask the following questions when offered a service, support, or specialized opportunity.

- How specifically does this _____ [service/therapy/support] benefit daily functioning and support our vision of capable?

- What is my child missing during this _____ [service/therapy/support]?

- Does the benefit of this _____ [service/therapy/support] outweigh the cost in lost time or opportunities?

Other tempting trade-offs

By second grade the occupational therapist was convinced that my son would never write with his hand. She proposed an adaptive technology tool called the Alphasmart, a compact keyboard that would digitally produce all of Jack's writing for him. It was tempting. Jack's hand muscles tired easily, his writing was illegible, and at nearly eight years old he was still most comfortable holding his pencil or crayon whole-fisted. And bonus, he was, like all kids his age, a technology native who loved pecking away on computer keys. His case manager spread the icing on the cake when she said, "It was the team's opinion that Jack wouldn't be able to keep up with notetaking as he moved into the upper elementary grades and middle school." And then she added the cherry on top: "And Mrs. Winking, if you think about it, printing or writing by hand does not matter because we all do everything on computers these days."

I indulged the prospect of not having to endure Jack complaining when he had to handwrite assignments, and considered how he would love all the bells and whistles on the Alphasmart.

Experience has taught me to neither accept nor refuse a service blindly.

After this convincing pitch, I had almost signed off on the IEP amendment sealing the deal authorizing the Alphasmart and extra time for learning to use it. But something unnamed kept gnawing at me. Instead of rushing in to accept the tool, I paused and considered our future vision for Jack. I imagined him in a job that he liked someday and living independently. Surely he would have to sign paychecks (remember this was 2005) and leave notes for his roommates, whoever they might be. I contemplated the irony that all the people on the team saying that Jack did not need to be able to write with his hand because of the preeminence of technology were actually sitting in the meeting writing notes or doodling on paper. On top of all of this, the kid loved stories—listening to them, creating them, reading them. He had a lot to say to the world, and I wanted him to have the choice to express his thoughts on paper or on the computer—if that was possible. On second thought, I would not sign off on the Alphasmart. I was not about to let the allure of this slick technology tool and the prospect of an easier life for Jack in the short run take away his options down the road.

The IEP team did a little head-scratching, but reluctantly accepted my decision. Instead we went with a program that taught handwriting and printing using an adaptive method. I compromised by saying that I was okay with Jack using the Alphasmart to "rewrite" assignments but that he should continue his handwriting instruction. It was important that we had not closed any doors; not traded our son's long-term potential for the expediency of what appeared, at the time, to be an easy answer for him and his teachers.

Life is a series of small decisions, many made unconsciously or with very little thought. There are natural points during the course of childhood, particularly for kids with disabilities when decisions are made to abandon one goal for another; for example, abandoning academic reading for survival reading or exchanging the curriculum necessary for a standard diploma with one focused on community access. Be aware of "skill trade-offs" you may be making unintentionally when you agree to services, modifications, or various technologies for your child. Be a critical consumer of therapies based on your vision of capable for and with your child.

Planning to phase out to maximum independence

Consider everything in light of the vision of capable. Once a service or support is established, ensure that there is a plan from the outset for how competencies will be maintained over time as supports are phased out. If your child requires 1:1 support to get to class, insist from the start that criteria are established for fading these external supports by explicitly teaching environmental cues or other strategies that your child can come to manage over time. Even if your child requires a particular support long-term, identify how your child will systematically increase his agency or independence in using the support. For example, control of a communication device may initially be in the teacher's hands but should transition to the child as they mature. It may be written in the IEP that the instructional aide packs the child's backpack, but the initial plan should also include how the child takes increasing responsibility for their backpack and materials over time.

To label or not to label, that is the question

As our kids mature, grow in skills, and gain self-monitoring strategies, it is fair to consider the role that their special education label serves. The goal of special education should be maximum learning and independence—which necessarily looks different for every child, but should always include a progression of support with accommodations, progressive goals, self-management of behavior, fading support, and intentionally moving toward autonomy. Maximum independence varies by individual. It may mean managing one's own self-care and hygiene routines, initiating friendships using an assistive communication device, spending part of the school day in general education classes, learning full-time in the general education classroom with supports, or complete exit of the special education system.

As we continue to identify children with extraordinary needs and intervene at younger ages, the mindset of a responsible special educator should always be to work themself out of the job. That is, as the student becomes more independent, is taught to use accommodations and workarounds, and masters strategies for maintaining learned skills, reliance on the special educator and external support should decrease.

Independent learning and autonomy should be the special education "North Star." Whether that best happens within or outside of a special education label depends on the individual child. To *evolve* toward maximum learning and independence is the goal, not *getting out* of special education. However, to the extent that the system itself is holding a student back from achieving independence, getting out becomes the de facto goal. As long as a student is benefiting from special education support, it makes sense to continue that support. But special education should never be a foregone conclusion. In fact, for too many kids, special education labels become self-fulfilling prophecies—the longer they are receiving services and support the more they rely on them. That is why I strongly encourage parents to ensure that every support or service that is added to an IEP includes from the outset a plan for fading it to maximum independence (whatever that looks like for the individual). As the supports and scaffolds triggered by the label and erected by the system are no longer needed, they should be questioned and gradually dismantled so that ultimately the child maintains autonomy and agency for their learning. Logically it follows that for some children this means exiting special education altogether.

As soon as they are able, involve your child in all IEP meetings and decisions. When this starts will vary based on your child's development age and maturity. Even if they are not able to participate in decision-making, include your child in meetings. Require them to participate in determining their own destiny. Parents may be able to request that their child is trained to lead their IEP meeting. In the United States, this practice of student-led IEPs is observed in most districts to some extent and includes requiring that students know their goals and take responsibility for meeting them, that they know and can show where they are in their learning with numbers (grades or test scores) or portfolios of their work, and that they are accountable for their progress. Student-led IEPs are one of the best ways to ensure that the goal for your child remains independence and autonomy.

Seek out challenging learning environments

Raising a child to be capable involves choice and intentionality. Children are always taking in new stimuli through their senses and in that way they are always learning. However, children without disabilities are generally more inclined to pick up new skills naturally, "learning incidentally" they call it. Incidental learning looks like this: After watching neighborhood kids riding bikes, your five-year-old hops on a two-wheeler and takes off wobbling down the sidewalk. Your youngest child grips the crayon with a tripod grasp because that is how he sees his older brothers and sisters do it. You marvel as you watch your kindergartner with his pointer finger poised over a printed page, picking out individual words as he reads to the dog.

Our children with disabilities are learning all the time too, but for the most part progress for them happens on purpose, not by accident. Even more than "neurotypical" kids, they require environments that invite learning, that offer opportunities for repeated practice, that draw their attention to relevant learning tasks, and that consistently challenge them in positive ways to take part in the learning.

Children who are delayed need more challenge, not less.

Low expectations, rigid routines, crowded classrooms, and vast differences in student needs are engagement killers. I admit I loved the teachers who loved my child, but love and care alone will not cut it for the majority of our kids. Our kids require intentional engagement and challenge. Even when they are not directly damaging your child, environments that are not engaging and that lack challenge are a waste of precious learning and development time.

Make time to visit your child's classroom. Notice how learning is happening. Are learning materials and resources intentionally set up for children to access them on their own? Are children getting what they need to independently explore new challenges, or are they sitting waiting to have learning served up to them? Are adults hovering over students, jumping in "to help" in order to stay on schedule, or are they letting students try, adjust, and try again with support as a new skill is built? Are there so many children with disparate needs that learning experiences are short-circuited because of a lack of time? Or is a slavish adherence to schedule honored over the learning that is taking place in the moment?

Be on the lookout for environments that offer the appropriate level of challenge and that prize intentional learning over schedule, structure, and control of materials.

In an elementary classroom this might look like teachers only offering students who have proven that they "can do it" the opportunity to handle the scissors (even though they are child-safe scissors). In middle school it is the kids who are allowed to sit on the sidelines of their collaborative learning group and those who are allowed to opt out of learning as long as they are not "bothering" anyone. By high school it looks like students waiting passively for papers to be passed out one by one, or kids being allowed to sit unengaged until the teacher "notices" they are without a sharpened pencil and gets them one. Parents who are raising their kid to be capable look for environments where the adults in charge are acting as facilitators of learning, not as gatekeepers who are holding the keys.

REFLECT...

* ...on how your child learns best:

  - What are your child's cognitive/academic strengths?

  - How can you leverage these strengths to shape the behavior you want to see?

  - How does each objective on your child's IEP support improved academic, behavioral, or social functioning?

* ...on the role of services and supports:

  - Have special services created unintended dependencies or deficits for your child? What are they?

  - In light of your shared vision of capable, imagine a support, service, accommodation, or piece of technology you might not accept for your child.

  - What trade-offs are you (and your child) accepting when you agree to specific supports and services in your child's IEP?

  - If your child was not spending time on this service, could that time be used for another service, activity, or experience that is of greater value given your goals?

  - What learning opportunities is your child missing out on because of this support? What natural processes are short-cut?

* ...on seeking challenging learning environments:

  - How much time does your child wait to be "served up" learning or developmental play activities?

  - What regular learning processes are being short-circuited

for expectancy and/or scheduling sake? How is the class-room set up for your child to take initiative?

- What message do you think your child is receiving from ongoing therapy and how might it shape her beliefs about herself and her abilities?

TRY IT ON...

- Use the "partnering with professionals" process to ensure that your child's IEP is aligned with your shared vision of capable.

  a. *Observe your child's learning and behavior.* Pay attention to how they learn and behave at different times of the day and in different settings.

  b. *Talk with your child about what works for them.* Ask questions and communicate with your child about what feels good to them when they are learning, what helps them focus, and what makes them want to work harder and spend time with others.

  c. *Clearly communicate the vision of capable to the team.* Share with the team the vision of capable you hold with your child (see Habit #3) as well as the support and services you believe your child needs to reach that vision.

  d. *Agree on the desired outcome with the team (the what).* Come to agreement with the IEP team on what the desired outcomes of services is. Ensure that it is written into the relevant section of the IEP.

  e. *Consider alternatives for meeting the desired outcome (the how).* Listen to the team, restate possible concerns to make sure you understand them, and be open to creative ways to meet the desired outcome.

f. *Agree on a plan to meet desired outcomes.* Agree on a plan and a schedule for review. Be prepared to revise the plan as necessary—the "how" can vary as long as it does not compromise the "what."

- Find a trusted teacher or therapist and talk with them to peel back labels and demystify terminology around your child's label/diagnoses. Where do these terms ring true in describing your child's learning, behavior, and communication patterns? And where do they fall short? Identify your child's special interests (e.g., trains, weather patterns, etc.) as well as strengths in specific learning skills and process areas (e.g., seeing in pictures, reading, technology, etc.). Use these to encourage the academic behavior you want to see.

- Help your child gain self-knowledge about how they best learn. Get into the habit of calling out what you notice in the moment and asking thoughtful questions to help your child get in touch with and internalize how they feel when they are learning.

- Take stock of your child's IEP. Review each support and service and ensure there is an intentional plan for phasing out. Take out a copy of your child's IEP or look at it online. Discuss each service, accommodation, and support that is written in your child's IEP. Analyze line by line the intent of each academic, occupational, behavioral, or speech objective. Ask yourself the question for each support or accommodation: "What is the plan to get my child to independence in this area?"

- Devise your own DIY therapy to accelerate your child's progress toward goals. Scan the environment for everyday activities and tasks that address formal occupational, physical, and speech therapy goals. Choose one and commit to using multiplying practice with this activity to supplement scheduled therapy.

- Request to sit in on one specialized service or support that your child receives. Note the specific skills and processes that it addresses. Reflect on how the service or support addresses your child's needs. Talk with the therapist about how the skills can be maintained over time as the service or support is reduced.

Allow Your Child to Make Choices and Experience the Consequences of Those Choices

GRAY AREAS

For Ronnie life was blissfully black and white, made up solely of things she wanted and things she didn't. That is why her parents, Mark and Shannon, were not overly surprised the day she declared with a dramatic flourish that she would go to Southwestern Junior College and become a nurse. This was not the inclusive college program specifically designed to support neurodiversity which they had dutifully researched, but Southwest Junior, a small regional college with a strong nursing program. Next Ronnie announced that she would live in the dorms.

With mixed emotions and a furrowed brow, Mark's response was "Go for it!" Because of Ronnie's complicated medical history, she had spent an inordinate amount of time in the company of nurses and had become fascinated with rare diseases. It made sense that she would be drawn to nursing. And why not? After all, she had gotten passing grades in geometry and biology in high school. Mark and Shannon's thinking was: "We don't know her limits, especially when it comes to something she is passionate about." They didn't see it as their job to cap Ronnie's potential. They would let the demands of a rigorous nursing program make that call...if it had to be made.

The plan behind the plan was "go for it—with support." Ronnie had a federally mandated "504 plan" which ensured that she could take all her tests untimed and in a 1:1 setting. Mark and Shannon worked with Southwest Junior to ensure that not only the counselor and transition coordinator but also the resident assistants (RAs) in her dorm would keep a close eye on Ronnie. Ronnie had passion and creativity in spades. But they knew all too well these same strengths could prove a double-edged sword when Ronnie's passions led her to obsessing, hoarding food, lying, and manipulating gray areas.

Once on campus, Ronnie started out strong. She got involved in theater and performed in two shows. In her signature role, she posed and preened in hot pink curls while her onstage angel serenaded her with an impressive rendition of "Beauty School Dropout." A dancer, like her mom, Ronnie searched out classes and even offered to pay RAs to take her to modern dance and ballet classes. She maintained decent grades, earning an impressive C+ in her pre-nursing anatomy class.

All seemed to be going well until Mark began to sense that Ronnie was being evasive on calls home. He and Shannon both caught Ronnie in half truths about how she was spending her free time—benign maybe, but looking back her parents recognized this as Strike One. Strike Two came when the counselor called to report that Ronnie was telling friends that she was hearing voices that were telling her to take roommates' shampoos, conditioners, and personal care products. Not long after, Mike intercepted a text revealing that Ronnie had been communicating with and attempting to meet a stranger while using the online handle of "Toilet Ghost Queen."

For Ronnie, this was all a perfectly innocent fantasy game born out of her love of characters from the *Harry Potter* novels, specifically Moaning Myrtle of Hogwarts bathroom fame. The problem was that the anonymous individual on the other end of the game did not share Ronnie's virtuous intent. For Mark and Shannon this was a hard Strike Three.

They told Ronnie to pack up her things; she was coming home. The risks were real and so were the consequences. Ronnie was without her phone and would not return to Southwest Junior anytime soon.

Shannon and Mike witnessed their daughter thrive in so many ways and don't regret letting Ronnie make the choice to go off to college.

"She showed us, but more importantly she showed herself, that she could get to classes on her own every morning, maintain her grades, and seek out friends and social activities."

Back at home now, Ronnie has time to connect the consequence of withdrawal from college with *her* actions, *her* choices. She is coming to realize that dishonesty with her parents, breaking the rules when no one was looking, and taking advantage of her newfound freedom did not work out for her and was definitely not safe. After the appropriate margin of sulking time expected of any 19-year-old, she has turned her attention to a new passion—volunteering at the local animal shelter. Mark and Shannon are proud of the fact that Ronnie is exploring the world of work and focusing on a new goal. One complete with its own set of choices and new learnings that will arise from those choices.[1]

Ronnie's story explained

Ronnie, no doubt, would have been safer if her parents had called the shots, but then they would have robbed her of the dignity and maturation that comes with charting one's own course. They and Ronnie may have never discovered all she was capable of.

Ronnie's parents tamed their fears in light of their vision of capable and allowed her to make a choice that aligned with *her* interests, not theirs. They gave her the power, advanced her agency, even as they acknowledged their concerns. They put scaffolds in place: the 504 plan, the regular check-ins with the counselor, transition coordinator, and RA, and of course the frequent phone calls from home. Ronnie's choice went sideways in potentially terrifying ways, as is always possible particularly when an inexperienced chooser is at the wheel.

This is scary for parents, but is it any more scary than the hit Ronnie's quality of life and sense of self would have taken had she not experienced the satisfaction that came with walking her own path as well as the learning that came as a result of her choices? Admittedly, this was only one crossroads in Ronnie's young life, but if denied choice and consequence over the long haul we know the outcomes for

1   Ronnie has Prader-Willi syndrome.

kids are not good. For it is in the wake of choices and consequences that we pat ourselves on the back or dust ourselves off and move forward—bruised but wiser.

In addition to building personal agency and self-determination, if Ronnie's parents had played it safe, they would have robbed their daughter of building a body of self-knowledge. Knowledge that it was *her* efforts that got *her* signed up for dance classes, into the musical, and earned her a C+ in anatomy. Not an inconsequential side benefit, Ronnie's parents would not have known how capable their daughter was.

The Habit: Capable parents make sure that their child has ample opportunities to make choices and experience the consequences of those choices. They are aware that giving their child this freedom comes with some peril. Our children mature asynchronously, most struggle to master the executive functions necessary to make thoughtful choices. Capable parents see this as all the more reason for them to be intentional in giving their child opportunities to practice choice-making. They will make good ones and bad ones and they will incur pain. However, these parents recognize the deeper, long-lasting wound of choosing for their child. They know that it is the dignity that we get from making our own choices and experiencing their consequences that makes us fully human in ways that transcend neurodivergence.

THE SCIENCE BEHIND THE HABIT

Humans are not born good decision-makers, we learn to be. It is through experiencing both the barbs of miscalculation and the bliss of self-satisfaction that we forge the neural pathways that make us better choice-makers.

Making choices involves gathering information, assessing alternatives, recognizing trade-offs, and reconciling oneself to the (sometimes ugly) fallout of our decisions. Giving children choices helps them feel like they have some degree of power and control over what they do. It's a necessary step in growing up as an autonomous being.

It is successive opportunities to make choices overlaid throughout the course of a childhood that allows us to mature with a sense of agency. The dictionary defines agency as the capacity to act to exert power or influence. Practically speaking, agency is the sense of control we feel to influence our own thoughts and behavior, to chart our own course in this world. Believing that we have some say over our lives helps us maintain a sense of calm in the face of change or when things don't go as planned. Regardless of the challenges they face, our children with disabilities need to experience this choice-making/consequence-feeling cycle and the dignity that comes with it.

Flexing those choice-making muscles

A subset of adults presiding over the current generation have been particularly criticized for over-rescuing their children. They even have their own name, "helicopter parents," describing their penchant for hovering over their kids to spare them the pain and discomfort of life. This general attitude toward rescue has fed practices like "every kid on the team gets a trophy" (we can't risk anyone feeling left out) and "kindergartners need a cellphone" (I need to be in touch with my kid at all times) that are now becoming the scapegoats for what observers are perceiving as a less resilient generation of young people. The jury is still out over whether this is true writ large, and we must concede that history has shown that every generation finds faults in the generations that follow.

It is true, however, that "helicoptering" has been with us long enough to have been researched. Studies show that this brand of parenting lowers kids' sense of self-efficacy and can lead to self-esteem issues, anxiety disorders, and even depression (Vigdal and Brønnick 2022).

Whatever the scourge of helicopter parents, the regular course of childhood in most societies is set up to dole out increased responsibility to our "typically" developing kids almost as a matter of course as they grow. Every step from choosing their preferred color of play dough, to deciding on extracurricular activities, to shaping "the look" they want to sport in high school (jock, gothic, techie, cosplay, etc.), to if and how they want to earn extra cash (fast food, landscaping, baby- or dog-sitting), to the type of course load they decide to take on (regular, honors, or advanced placement), helps them flex their decision-making muscles.

Even if grownups are putting a thumb on the scales to some extent, the child is still getting practice at weighing options, comparing alternatives, and reconciling the trade-offs that come with making choices. For example, "I chose the blow-off class and I was bored" or "I tried chess club and I really liked it." When regularly engaging in this process over time children become accustomed to the fact that consequences are just a part of choices freely made. Making peace with outcomes they don't like is not easy for any kid, but over time they come to expect them.

Even when we choose badly we still have the satisfaction that we had a voice, we exercised *our* will. It is the cycle of decision-making repeated over and over again that molds us. Albert Camus, philosopher and Nobel Laureate, said, "Life is the sum of all your choices." Who are we if we are not allowed a say in those life-defining moments?

Too often this cycle that develops agency and literally shapes our complex personalities is short-circuited for kids who have disabilities. Sadly, choice-making is even more constricted the greater the perceived disability.

We rob our children of agency when we give them false choices or options that are not relevant to their lives. We exempt them from choices because we don't think they are capable. We choose for them because they may not have been reliable choosers in the past. We pick for them when they are slow to decide and circumstances demand that we adults move things along.

Robbed of agency

Children who are consistently not allowed to make their own choices because of parental fear, concern for safety, or expediency become less present in their own lives. Let's face it, if you are not given a say in the choice, you have a different relationship to the consequences.

Put yourself in our kids' shoes. You might not particularly like that ice cream flavor, that movie, those shoes, or that game. They all just "happened to you," landed on you through no action of your own. The next time you might exert your will by toppling the cone onto the pavement, turning away from the movie, throwing those shoes, or flopping to the ground to avoid having to join the game. All of these are acts of volition for sure, and good for you! But they do nothing to make you a better decision-maker in the future.

On the other hand if *you* chose the too-salty, salted caramel ice cream, the overly scary movie, the uncomfortable shoes, or the unfun game, it is on you. It is consequences—the lingering salty taste in your mouth, the bad dream you can't forget, the blisters on your feet, or the memory of sitting on the sidelines during the game—that begin to etch pathways in your brain. The next time you may flex your decision-making muscles in a different direction. That is agency!

APPLYING THE HABIT

Make choices clear, safe, and progressively more sophisticated

Giving kids choices can be risky, but assuming some degree of risk builds confidence and teaches other valuable life skills like self-regulation. No parent is going to let a child who struggles with overstimulation, who cannot intuitively judge the velocity of an oncoming car, or understand the meaning of traffic signals, choose when to cross the street. That is not safe. Depending on our child's developmental level and their ability to make sense of environmental cues, we provide varying levels of scaffolds to assist in their decision-making. Regardless of the level of their challenges we can and should intentionally build in opportunities for all our kids to make choices and see their way through the consequences.

Choices are all around us, just waiting for you to offer them to build skills, agency, and self-knowledge. You can offer "what," "when," "who," and "where" choices for your child. "What" choices can help children develop informed preferences—like determining their favorite toys, movies, and games. "What" choices can also help introduce new foods or experiences. Just having the power of choice encourages us to try something new or tolerate an anxiety-producing activity. Whether it is selecting what goes in their lunchboxes or determining what song to listen to while in the shower, choice is enticing.

"When" choices can help teach a child to learn to wait, delay one thing for another, and learn about "trade-offs"—an indispensable life skill. "You can play on the iPad until dinner or play after, but not both...you choose." "We eat a sweet treat once a day, do you want ice cream now or do you want to wait until after therapy?"

"Where" choices can give kids some control around their sensory environment and help them gain self-knowledge about what surroundings help them focus on various activities. "Would you like to do your homework in the beanbag chair, at the desk in your room, or in the kitchen?" Choice builds relevance and fun into tasks that have to get done. You pick your favorite song to listen to while you clean up the Legos or the specific dish you want to help cook. As your child gets more and more practice flexing those decision-making muscles, add options and emphasize key trade-offs.

The mere act of choice-making leads to self-knowledge. However, since individuals with disabilities often struggle with thinking about their thinking (metacognition), work with your child as much as possible to get them to reflect on choices they have made. Pause and ask them what they liked and didn't like, how they felt after they made their choice, and what surprised them. Depending on developmental level and how in touch they are with their feelings your child may need to experience the consequences of their choice multiple times to make the connection. Fourteen-year-old Sadie used her communication device to choose "screen time before dinner" and now faces a long evening with no iPad. Her mom helps her make the connection by putting the iPad away on the shelf above the refrigerator as Sadie watches, by offering other activities (but not screens), and by using declarative statements like "We can read or go outside" or "You chose no iPad after dinner," and asking questions such as "How does it feel to read together after dinner?" She pauses for Sadie to respond on her device. "If it does not feel good, next time choose iPad after dinner instead."

Loving limits

Leaders in the area of "peaceful discipline" advocate for teaching kids limits, and not imposing consequences (Moore 2022). It looks like positively describing the boundaries around what a child *can* do instead of focusing on the negative things that will happen if they *fail* to operate within the boundaries.

Taking the time necessary to offer your child choices is a genius move because it not only helps with decision-making, it is also a great way to teach limits. It is a twofer because the act of making a choice defines the limit. "You can have this or this, but not both," "You can play now or later, but not at both times," "You can ride here or there, but not anywhere you want to."

Consequences clarified—intentions matter

We can get stuck thinking of consequences as a bad thing. But actually consequences come in both flavors, positive and negative. While we don't want to see our child in pain, we need them to feel both types—it is experiencing both that makes us fully human.

To complicate matters, consequences whether good or bad come in two types, natural and imposed. We don't put our homework in our backpack, the teacher can't grade it, our grade is lower (natural consequence). In this case we do not intervene, the consequence happens as a matter of course after the choice. Mom says no movie tonight for not loading our backpack (imposed consequence). In this case, mom has intervened, the consequence is imposed, and it is not directly related to the choice.

It is important to note that while natural consequences can be the most powerful, they only work if the individual cares—if an A and F mean the same to my child, the natural consequence of a lower grade is ineffective and won't change their homework-turning-in behavior one bit.

Discipline literally means "teaching or instruction." While natural consequences are the bomb *when they matter to a child* (e.g., missing a fun activity because they are late, getting cold when they refuse to wear long pants in the winter, and getting sick because they ate too much Halloween candy), imposed consequences are not useless, they can also teach in a positive way—it all depends on how the child reads our intention.

There is much being made of loss of privileges in current parenting literature. The thought is that loss of a privilege (a phone, an iPad, videogame time, a trip to the amusement park, or a favorite toy) is a consequence that sends a negative message in that it teaches your child that you (the adult) can inflict pain on them by removing something that they love or enjoy. But in fact how the child sees a consequence depends on your intention and how effectively and empathetically you are able to communicate that intention.

Children can tell the difference between, on the one hand, their parents feeling angry, resentful, or upset and using that emotion to "teach them a lesson" and, on the other hand, their expressing genuine concern, love, and wishing good things for them. Note the difference in intention in each: "You didn't do your laundry when I told you to, so I am taking your Xbox away for the rest of the week" and "I am worried that the Xbox is getting in the way of you getting your laundry done; I know you like clean clothes for school, so I will hang on to the controller just until you get the washer started"; or "I am taking that Furby because you turned in a blank math page!" and "Your blank math page makes me think you need more help to focus; I am worried that taking care of your Furby is consuming all your attention, so help me find a place to put it up until you are done with math"; or "You hit your little sister, so you don't get to play with her!" and "You hitting your little sister makes me think you are frustrated now and that you will feel better playing together after a little time apart."

It cannot be repeated enough, children understand our tone of voice well before they understand our words. Regardless of their developmental level your child is expert at detecting and responding to a loving attitude and the tone of voice that accompanies it; just as they can detect anxiety or dysregulation in our demeanor.

When consequences are short-circuited

I spend a lot of time with families who are living the pain born out of a pattern of ensuring that there are consequences and limits for their neurotypical child(ren) but not for their child who is neurodivergent. When parents look inward, they find the main culprits for not allowing their child to experience consequences. They may feel sorrow or pity for their child, misplaced guilt around their child's disability, or that it is just too painful (for their child or them) to allow the consequences or limits to stand.

I am the last one to judge as I have been there myself. The thinking goes something like this: "So much is hard in life for this child, let's not allow this to be hard too. He is just going to tantrum if I remind him it is time to move off technology and that is sure to set everyone in the house off." If you have been in my shoes, failing to maintain consequences or let limits stand for your child with a disability, you are not alone. Ask yourself why. Return to Habit #5 and do the work to name the fears that lead you to not imposing limits in the first place or not allowing your child to bump up against them once you have set them.

Allowing your child to feel consequences is painful at first, but your child and everyone in the house will bounce back. Look at your fears through the lens of your vision of capable, and nine times out of ten you will see that your child has more to lose in the long run when you protect them from consequences or when you don't adhere to limits.

Inexpensive lessons—priceless learning

When our kids don't experience consequences they come unprepared to the next step in life, whatever that is. With Habit #3 we identify a sound vision of capable with our child. Even with that vision in place, for a whole host of reasons, including frequent transitions, lack of consistent services, an unacceptable shortage of adult living options, and high unemployment and underemployment within the disabled and neurodivergent communities, the next step for our child can feel unsure, unreal, almost like a pipe dream.

Sam dreamed of doing illustration. He had a creative brain. Seeing in pictures gave him a knack for digital rendering. Pathological Demand Avoidance or Pervasive Drive for Autonomy (PDA) associated with his spectrum disorder caused him to opt out of anything he viewed as a demand, and the self-absorption common to 19-year-olds the world over caused him to focus his time almost exclusively on what he wanted to do. When he did not get in the car for high school many mornings or logged out halfway through online classes, his parents did not impose limits. Accommodations on his IEP exempted him from the typical consequences of not showing up for school. When he lost interest in learning the public transit schedule, his mom drove him to restaurants and the mall. Then came time for the next step. Sam's transition plan required him to log in for mock job interviews and show up on time for job-shadowing opportunities at various companies. Sam was unprepared to move toward his vision because he did not know that professional interviewers would log off if he did not show up on screen on time, or that job-shadow opportunities would dry up after the first or second time he didn't show up. Sam and his parents were suffering from a long history of consequences deferred.

No parent wants their child to age out of school at 18 or 21 without having had the opportunity actively to practice making choices about his life, feeling consequences, and advocating for himself. These experiences are necessary whether our child's next step is to be able to ask a community college faculty member for an accommodation or an employer for a raise, to follow the rules of their group home, or to communicate their preferences so they get to attend community outings offered by their adult service program.

Holding fast on limits is hard. Whenever our child gets sideswiped by natural consequences, it hurts us too. We feel our child's pain keenly. However, the cost of limits and consequences felt by our child when they are young is minuscule compared with when they are older. Our shared vision of capable with our child may shift over time and based on circumstances; but if we adhere to that vision, we soon see the lessons of limits and experiencing consequences are an important part of moving to almost every vision.

JACK'S STORY—THE LATE BIRD IS LEFT HOLDING THE SHOVEL

Jack had some form of summer work since he was 14, whether cutting grass or stocking supermarket shelves. The summer of his 18th year, there was no automatic job to fall into, no neighbor who asked if he could tend to their yard, and no friend of ours at the recreation center who could slide him into a slot. We reminded Jack that if he did not start looking, all the "good jobs" would be gone. We were conflicted, we knew his communication disfluencies and cognitive-processing difficulties were causing him to drag his feet. These were real challenges. On the other hand, early on we had offered to help, supplied contacts, and gave ideas; supports were there. He chose to avoid checking into all the usual summer employers. By the time he got around to looking, the only option left was bottom rung on the food chain with a local landscaping crew. This was grueling work in the hot sun that taxed his physical limits.

It had taken years of therapy to build core strength, motor planning, balance, and core strength. Even so, Jack tended to wilt in heat and humidity. Still torn, a part of us longed to swoop in and rescue him. But we held back, supporting him by making overstuffed sandwiches and offering big jugs of drinking water and high-SPF sunscreen. We had real fears about how his body would respond to such work. But Jack made his choice to avoid the job search process and that summer learned a universal truth that "the early bird gets the worm, and the guy who doesn't look for a job ends up digging holes." Message received, he experienced the consequences of procrastination and has worked hard since to make himself qualified for work jobs that don't require back-breaking labor.

We believed that there was dignity to be found in making choices and accepting the risk inherent in those choices. It would short-circuit the entire learning process for Jack if we only let the consequences stand when they were positive and went his way. Hard knocks were a part of life, and insulating our son from them would relieve him of short-term pain but would rob him of lifelong dignity.

When you don't intervene and let your child make their own choices, whether big or small, sometimes they will get hurt. (This is true even when you have given them the tools you think they will need.) But they also get something else. They get the message, loud and clear, that you, the most influential person in their life, trust them and believe they are capable.

This pattern repeated itself many times during Jack's childhood, where he made choices that put him in situations that were risky or with people who might hurt him. We learned the important truth that protecting your child from challenging situations or making choices for them may avoid triggering your own fears, but it will also rob your child of the experiences they need to grow and view themselves as autonomous beings.

REFLECT...

- How do you regularly help your child flex their decision-making muscles?

- Do you let your child experience the natural consequences of their actions?

- What kinds of choices do you allow/encourage your child to make?

- What kinds of choices don't you allow them to make?

- What makes you fearful for your child?

- What do you imagine would happen if one of those fearful situations occurred?

- What would be the consequences for you? For your child?

- Think of a time when your child encountered a limit or experienced a consequence as a result of their choices or behavior. Did you allow them to experience the consequence or did you intervene? How did your child react? What would you do the same or different next time?

TRY IT ON...

- Help your child practice flexing their choice-making muscles.

  Offer your child a choice. After they have made the choice and experienced what the choice resulted in, pause and spend some time asking them questions and making declarative statements that help them reflect on their choice. Did they like the result of their choice? What surprised them? What would they do different next time if they had to make the decision again?

  Based on their responses, identify what else you can do to get them to think more about their choices.

- Create a limit and let it stand. Reflect on how it feels for you and your child.

  Identify an area where your child could benefit from a limit (e.g., "iPad before dinner or after but not both," "We play with stuffy bear during quiet time, but not during play group," "Ear buds are good for free time but not at the dinner table," etc.). Set the limit. Note how your child responds. Maintain the limit over a couple of weeks, note how your child's response changes over time.

Celebrate Your Child's Persistence
to Build a Narrative of Strength

TAKE A PICTURE—IT LASTS LONGER

Request almost any song, Jensen can play it. He taught himself to read music and has been invited to be a busker, playing for patrons at the local farmer's market. The problem is his working memory just doesn't work. Because of seizures during infancy which culminated in a stroke, Jensen experiences confounding memory deficits. On the one hand, he is a star player on the unified basketball team; on the other hand, he is confused and anxious about where to position the faucet controls to get his bath to a bearable temperature.

His memory challenges have triggered a significant anxiety disorder, which has become a vicious cycle. Since most things, even those he has done before, feel brand new to Jensen, he is understandably wary of them. For Jensen controlling his environment has been his best defense to decrease the unpredictability that provokes fear and anxiety.

Ericka, his mom, explains it this way: "It would take days to coax Jensen into going to the waterpark. Once there he would have a great time horsing around with his dad. A couple of weeks later we'd announce that we were heading to the waterpark again and he would resist because he had no memory of the experience." Jensen's entire family has worked hard to help him create a track record of all he has accomplished. In middle school his aunt got him a camera and encouraged him to take photos. Jensen would review the photos over and over as a living color tribute of all the things he had done and challenges he had mastered.

At 16, Ericka suggested that they take a four-mile bike trip to the next town, get ice cream, and ride back. Jensen became extremely anxious, complaining that it was too hard. After first acknowledging his fear, Ericka said, "Come on, you have done hard things before, and you always feel good after you do them. Trust that your body knows what to do, your brain is just tricking you into thinking you can't."

Despite steep inclines and monotonous stretches of pavement, Ericka and Jensen completed that ride, snapping a proud selfie at the halfway point. That evening, not only the photo but sore hamstrings and a satisfied smile were undeniable proof to Jensen that he had prevailed...once again.[1]

The Habit: Capable parents celebrate their child's effort and use it to help their child build and internalize a personal narrative of strength. They know all too well that, in a world that prizes conformity and seeks to put a bright line distinction around difference, their child likely gets many more negative messages than positive ones. These parents intentionally seek to shift that balance by calling out their child's hard work, persistence, resilience, and determination rather than focusing on the details of what their kid gets "right or wrong" or how "fast" they get it done.

THE SCIENCE BEHIND THE HABIT

More than three decades of mindset research reminds us all that struggle is to be expected and embraced. It is the necessary fuel for our future successes. In fact, the real problem is not "struggle" but the emphasis on intelligence and talent. The implication is that smarts, physical agility, artistic skill, musical talent, and a whole host of traits are inborn and fixed. If you believe you've either "got it" or

1 Jensen has autism and short-term retrieval disorder.

"you haven't," you avoid challenges because they may reveal weakness. You are unmotivated to learn because learning inevitably involves risk and failure.

Researchers like Angela Duckworth (2018) and Carol Dweck (2007) have shown that we can teach children to have a "growth mindset," which focuses on the "getting there" rather than what you started out with in terms of raw material. With a growth mindset we seek out and embrace new learning and experiences. We are not afraid that challenges will expose us as losers, instead we know that each time we stare down a challenge or difficulty we become better, stronger, more agile, smarter, or whatever it is we want to be. A growth mindset produces higher achievers in school and in life.

It is hard to embrace learning challenges and expose yourself to intellectual risks when you are getting negative messages from your environment. Experts estimate that, by age ten, kids with ADHD receive 20,000 more negative comments than they do positive ones (Bogdanov 2023). Rejection hits us all hard. Research consistently shows that children with ADHD, ASD, and learning disabilities have lower self-esteem than their neurotypical peers.

Helping our kids create positive personal narratives can increase self-worth and becomes a reinforcing cycle that maintains a growth mindset into adulthood.

APPLYING THE HABIT

Reframing success

The old adage "Success breeds success" does not just make for snappy greeting cards and motivational posters, our children absolutely need internalized feelings of success piled up over time to view themselves as capable. But too often, particularly for kids with disabilities, their environment delivers just the opposite. Most of us would like to live in a universe with more shape and texture than a simple tally of winners and losers; a black-and-white world where a rigid definition of aptitude funnels us all into dichotomous categories of winners and losers. A better world is one where sincere effort is rewarded and where sweat produces equity.

We all want this for our children, but real life too often telegraphs subtle and not so subtle messages that get stacked up in plus and minus columns in our psyches. Mindset research gives us a framework for digesting those messages: Struggle is to be expected; it is the necessary fuel for future success. But how are those messages mediated within young minds?

From what I have seen, particularly for our kids who are neurodivergent, the internal columns assigned to wins and losses were tilted way too far toward the negative.

The tally

My son Jack had always struggled with self-esteem and I believed this "internal tally sheet" was in large part responsible for anger issues that I saw incubating as he grew. This is how, in his words, the tally stacked up for him:

> When I spoke and the kid next to me predictably rolled her eyes because she doesn't like how I look: loss. When the kids talk over me as if I am not there because there are too many "uhms" in my delivery: loss. When everyone finished the math work and got to go to free time with me still sitting there: loss. When classmates walk away as I am telling a story because it was taking too long for me to get the words out: loss. When the PE teacher tells the class to run around the track and I am trailing dead last: loss. When I whiff the ball and kick the air during the kickball game while everyone watches: loss. When the point I make in class repeats what another kid had just said because of the extra time it takes me to process my thoughts and a couple of kids snicker: loss. When the girl reading my paper says she can't read it because my handwriting is too "babyish": loss. When I shoot 500 baskets in my driveway only to sit on the bench the entire game as teammates fly down the court oblivious to my presence on the team: loss. When kids are going on about the party that everyone is invited to but me: loss. When the boys egged me on to drink hot

sauce at lunch because they knew I didn't have the confidence or guts to say no: loss. When my roommate at camp moves out with no explanation: loss.

If this was a heartbreaking paragraph to read, imagine how many of our children have these experiences every day, and then compound these experiences over the course of a childhood.

Tipping the balance

These messages, even when not intentionally cruel, are a powerful toxin to our child's self-worth. It is hard to preach the gospel of "effort matters more than ability" when you see your child sinking under the weight of this invisible tally sheet. How do we continue to encourage kids to engage and put themselves out there again and again in the face of such feedback?

The answer lies in continuing to build that growth mindset. First, we parents need to adopt and model a growth mindset for ourselves. We need to show it in how we react to difficulties, setbacks, frustrations in our own lives. Whether it be fixing something in the garage, cooking in the kitchen, or talking about our jobs, we need to show in our words and actions that we are more concerned with *what we are doing and the joy we are getting from it*, rather than the need to do whatever it is perfectly.

Beyond modeling, we mediate and minimize the negative messages our kids get by calling out and praising them for the process they are using or the part they are playing in a project or activity. This includes:

- their persistence at a task

- creative ideas or unique perspectives they contribute

- an unusual strategy they use to solve a problem

- the positive attitude they show

- how they encourage and cheer on others in their group

- their dogged pursuit of a solution even when it takes more time.

Each of these focuses on the effort they put in, the strategies they used, or the attitude they showed, and takes the focus off being the first or the smartest.

Over time we want to help our child rewrite the "traditional" success story by making it about persistence and resilience rather than getting an easy grade A. In our case, the weight of the negative messages that Jack received threaten to instill a fixed mindset of "I can't do anything right," "I am not likeable," "People don't think I have good ideas," "I am dumb," or "I am awkward."

Instead of focusing on what Jack got right about the outcome, I focused on what Jack got right about the process, which is much more important in the long game of life. We said things like "You know something about you, you always hang in there until the job gets done," "The coach said that she appreciates how you always cheer everyone on and build the team up," "You kept trying different ways until you got a solution, that is what successful people do," "I love how you figured out how to complete that project in a way that made sense for you," "You know you have made it to every single practice this year, even on tough days when a lot of other kids blew it off, that shows that you are a kid who does not give up," "Your teacher said you showed the new girl where her locker was, kindness like that pays off in life," "I noticed at the bus stop when everyone was making fun of Mrs. Collins, you did not join in, that says a lot about you."

When we actively "notice" and emphasize persistence, doing the right thing even when it is hard, curiosity, and trying new things, we teach our child that their brain is a learning machine that gobbles up challenges as its fuel. Staying safe and avoiding those things that at first blush seem difficult or demanding starves your brain. The message to your kid is "I can do hard things" and "persisting through trials is actually fun because it makes me better!"

Helping your child create their story

Depending on their development age and readiness, sometime during adolescence children begin to create stories for themselves. These stories are rooted in experience, and when kids tell themselves these stories over time they become entwined with their identity. This is what researchers call "narrative" identity (McLean 2005). To the extent that their cognitive functioning allows it, young people begin to see their past as something that they can make meaning out of. They use these reconstructions of their experiences as a way to help them understand where they are going in the future.

Your child might not be celebrated for being the "smartest," "strongest," "fastest," or "best"; however, when we notice and call out our child's persistence, grit, creativity, kindness, or patience, we are helping balance those negative messages. Focusing on effort will not take our child's pain away or erase the very real struggles they experience every day, but it will reframe them. We can help our kids build their own narrative of strength that will empower them rather than trap them into feeling like the victim of a story that others have "written" for them. While it can feel like small consolation in the moment, they will take this narrative with them through life and it will inform how they look at all the challenges still to come.

Finding their voice

Each of our children has a story of perseverance to tell. Through this process we hope our child finds their voice, however they communicate, and breaks through the noise to share with the world their unique gifts, talents, and perspectives. A friend's daughter who has autism and is a nonverbal communicator speaks with her art. Another young man I know communicates through the musical playlists he creates.

We raise them intentionally, sending them messages that we believe in them. But, in the end, they teach us infinitely more than we have ever taught them. My son definitely took me to school. I thought I had taught Jack a lot over the years, but in the end it was he who showed me what was truly important. The night I worried about what people would think of him as he prepared to share the story of his syndrome with an audience of his peers and their parents, he set me straight when he said, "You know, Mom, if they were going to think 'different' of me, I think they already have."

Put tests in their place

Standardized achievement tests do one thing really well. They quantify how much a child can "show" what they know on a particular subject on a particular date in time. Unless the particular test is repeated over and over, and allows students to respond in different ways, it does nothing to show growth over time or sustained knowledge.

> **Regardless of the principal's intentions, my child had been judged and sentenced based on his appearance and a 20-minute standardized test.**

Tests are not good predictors of success over the long haul. In fact a child's record of high school grades and course-taking patterns (measures of persistence and grit) are much better at predicting post-high school and college success than are standardized test scores (measures of point-in-time achievement), which rely on an outdated conceptualization of success. That is why universities, particularly in the United States, are moving away from such assessments.

Whether your child happens to be a good test taker or not, you are better off focusing on the *process* than on the score: "You worked so hard to get that score," "I noticed how you studied the harder material over and over." Because when we praise a score or a grade we encourage a fixed mindset: "If I am good when I get this score, I must *not* be good when I get less than that."

If and when tests are used with your child, make sure you know what they measure and what they do not. Be clear about what inferences can fairly be made based on each test. Far too often tests are used to make high-stakes decisions for which they were not designed.

REFLECT...

- What negative messages does your child regularly receive from his environment?

- What can you do to help him mediate those messages?

- How do you acknowledge the "bad" with your child?

- What messages do I send to my child that communicate that I believe he is capable, and what messages do I send that communicate otherwise?

- How might I change how I speak to and behave toward my child to send the message that I believe she is capable?

- What tests or assessment tools have been used to evaluate your child?

- How was the information from these tools used?

- How does your child react to disappointments?

- How do you react when your child experiences disappointment?

TRY IT ON...

- Any time a test is used with your child, make a point of asking testing professionals exactly what inferences (conclusions) can fairly be made based on the measure. Keep in mind what each test actually measures and what it does not.

  We can change the tally by reinforcing effort over "right or wrong." Experiences are logged as positive or negative and become part of our personal narrative.

- Make a point of calling out and recognizing your child's effort, creativity, character, or resilience. Observe how your child responds to disappointments. Identify areas in which you can recognize effort, creativity, character, or resilience over outcomes, "right or wrong," or the speed with which your child gets things done. Actively call these behaviors out to help your child to build a strong personal narrative.

Treat Yourself with Compassion, Make Mistakes, Laugh, and Learn from Them

WORKING WITHOUT A NET

Everything had gone according to plan. I had devised the game over a year ago when I had seen my son eyeing the banister. I had coaxed Jack up and on to it and was using it to build balance, motor planning, and that magical but elusive "core strength" that the physical therapists claimed he needed in order to take on all the other developmental milestones that lie ahead. The game started like this: I lifted him on so he was straddling the banister on his tummy, one arm and one leg dangling from either side. Holding my breath in anticipation, I shadowed my hands around his torso willing him to use his arms to inch himself up. At first...nothing.

Over time Jack went from lying limp on the slick varnished surface while I gingerly spotted him, to pulling himself onto and hugging the banister (sometimes with help, sometimes on his own), inching himself up hand over hand, and riding down. Success! My low-tone kid was climbing and sliding! Maybe it was only a couple of feet at a time... but still. I never tired of hearing that "Wheeeeee!" and seeing that killer smile as he giggled on the way down. "If you want to slide down, you have to climb high," I remember tempting him, counting on the increasing thrill of sliding a little further each time to entice him to work his slack arms and core muscles just a little more.

My physical therapy game was possible thanks to a cooperative floor plan. Our house had an open staircase. The floating banister that led to the second floor dropped off into the abyss of the family room on the main level, but it was that same openness that made it fair game for climbing.

I was proud of the game, until the morning a new friend and her little boy came over. Letting them in, I returned to the kitchen to attend to the stove. My friend let out a blood-curdling shriek upon seeing Jack precariously perched on the banister poised for a slide. This was just another Tuesday for us, but at this moment, my new friend was witnessing a child suspended nearly at the second floor on a thin railing, with only a couch partially covering the hardwood floor where his three siblings were playing below. This kid was working without a net! Inexplicably to her, the ringmaster of this crazy circus (me) didn't seem to care.

The sound drew me back into the scene, now viewing it through her eyes. She saw "risky, unsafe, undisciplined, and downright dangerous." I saw an important strength-training, motor-planning, and balance-building routine that was more interesting to my son than any structured PT session.

After the shriek came a mix of confusion and blame casting: "I would never let my kids do that," she offered out loud, as she attempted to remove Jack from the banister.

I caved. I threw my child under the bus. The need for acceptance caused me to betray my child to avoid letting my friend think of me as a "bad mom," negligent and endangering my child's life. I called out "What are you doing, Jack, get off that banister!" with a feigned mix of frustration and concern. Jack looked bewildered and a little sad. Mercifully, he did not "out" me, but his expression said it all. 'But Mom, you like the banister game, you even put me on it sometimes and make me do it.'

As the words escaped my mouth, I was already beating myself up. You *are* a bad mom, you yelled at your child for something you taught him and encouraged him to do. At best I had confused a kid who already received way too many mixed messages in life; and at worst I had shown him that I was dishonest; that I cared more about what other people thought than I cared about him.

The Habit: Capable parents treat themselves with compassion. They know they will make mistakes, and when they do they laugh and learn from them. They recognize that they can't take care of their child without taking care of themselves. This includes admitting they can't be everything for their child, getting vulnerable, letting go of situations and people who are shame-inducing, forgiving themselves, modeling for their child that mistakes are opportunities to learn, and making intentional time to recharge in ways that work uniquely for them.

THE SCIENCE BEHIND THE HABIT

It is a fact that the safer we feel as parents the more open and responsive we can be to our children. The problem is that when our child has been judged by society's yardstick as not quite "measuring up," we run into situations daily that threaten our safety. Even though disability awareness is evolving overall, in practice what we really have is an "awareness" of new vocabulary like "neurodivergence," "self-determination," and "disability agency." As a society we pat ourselves on the back for our mastery of new buzz words rather than getting down to the business of creating learning and living spaces which truly understand, honor, and work for *all* people regardless of difference.

Research has proven that self-compassion is not just a sappy-sounding platitude that we can throw around to let ourselves off the hook. It is essential to maintaining our mental health, allowing us to show up and respond positively to our child every day. When we look inward and judge ourselves with kindness rather than harshness, our body releases oxytocin, which increases feelings of calm, safety, and general connectedness (Uvnäs-Moberg, Handlin, and Petersson 2015).

Conversely, criticizing ourselves and harboring feelings that we are a "bad mom" or "bad dad" is perceived as a threat which kicks our reptilian brains into overdrive. In this state, we can't think carefully and we spend our time reacting to our child instead of responding in positive, purposeful ways.

It is only when we look at our whole selves, including our mistakes and reactions, with compassion, and when we actively practice strategies that "fill" our empty tanks, that we can show up for our child in ways that will help them reach that shared vision of capable. Capable parents know that they need to get Habit #12 right if they want to have any hope of internalizing the others.

APPLYING THE HABIT

On high alert

Too often parents of a child with a disability or who is neurodivergent live in a state of hypervigilance, ever on the lookout for the next looming threat. I remember tensing up as I drove up to the school thinking "I am dropping my kid off at a place that might reject him because of how he looks, moves, or responds." I swallow this first gut attack—but not really, it is still there. Then I head to work and switch on my laptop, only to learn that the internet is on fire with a new neuropsych treatment that everyone says works for kids just like mine. Does it work? Really? And if it does, how can I possibly afford one round of treatments, far less maintain it over time?

Later that same day, I learn my husband has been offered a great job but feel immediately selfish because I know moving will require my child to be reevaluated (again) and to start all over with a new batch of therapists. I am barely off the phone with my husband and I get the call about an IEP amendment meeting that needs to be scheduled for next week. Apparently the occupational therapist at school has determined that my kid's mouthing behavior is being increasingly seen as a hygiene concern in the classroom.

Looking forward to a quiet evening at home, I stop at the grocery store with my kids in tow to pick up dinner. After what I surmise must have been an overwhelming day at school, my kid flops to the ground between canned goods and the freezer aisle (again). I feel the shame rising within me as I start to lose it in public. I lay my head on the pillow that night with the murky outlines of yet to be imagined threats swirling in my brain. And tomorrow, I wake and do it all over again. And for some, this diary entry only scratches the surface of the emotional threats they experience on a regular basis.

Your child is resilient

Whether your child is two, 12, or 22, one of our greatest fears is that we won't be enough. That we are not up to the task of delivering what our child needs to succeed. This concern is amplified when the job of parenting turns out to be very different from what you thought it would be because of your child's birth story, neurodivergence, or disability.

In the banister story, I was ashamed of myself. I had not stood up for Jack, explained my belief that scaling banisters was good for this boy, a kind of supercharged physical therapy. I knew why I had not explained that it was I who had legitimized the sport of banister scaling in my home. I wanted my new friend to see Jack as an explorer, a little stuntman, caught up in the throes of "typical" boy behavior! I knew too well that I was reprimanding my kid because I wanted to save face with another adult. Again, not one of my proudest moments, but I knew I would be able to fix it with Jack. He would forgive his mother for this transgression, he may think it weird, but he would forgive me.

Being good to you is good for your child

How far can we run with this idea of being "good to ourselves"? Taken to the extreme it could look like chasing all forms of personal pleasure to numb fears and disconnect from all that is challenging about parenting. Roll tape of Hollywood caricatures: the absent dad who ships his child off to camp and maxes out child care to avoid the day-to-day grind of childrearing; or the power mom indulging in spa treatments, three martini lunches, nights out, and weekends away leaving the kids with the nanny.

Leaving La La Land and returning to reality, we realize the opposite is actually more common, particularly among parents raising a child with special needs. We run ourselves ragged trying to get our child the help they need. Drained, we then react out of overwhelm. We top it all off by beating ourselves up, promising to be better, to do better, in the future. This vicious cycle of trying to control things that are often out of our control, striving to the point of exhaustion, acting out, and then regretting it is self-reinforcing. It is a pattern that will repeat itself until we intentionally commit to being good to ourselves. When we finally do, we learn that taking breaks, and listening to what our body needs, has the effect of creating a stronger connection between us and our child rather than weakening it.

This Habit is not meant to provide an exhaustive compendium of self-care, but to instill the mindset that self-compassion is not optional but non-negotiable to successfully parenting all kids, and particularly kids with differences. These pages offer select strategies that we parents of children with disabilities can use to "get right" with ourselves and in doing so improve our relationship with our child and help them reach their full potential.

The enemy within

When our child looks, thinks, communicates, behaves, or moves in ways that fall outside the norm, our strong urge is to change our child. The assessment, the evaluation, the label, or the diagnosis screams what is "wrong" with our child. So we must do what we can to "fix" them.

Chances are we grew up in a time where conformity was prized, before the term "diversity" even included people with disabilities as a class worthy of consideration. Even though we love them intensely, what is "wrong" shouts louder, commanding our attention and drowning out the beautiful, unique, sensitive creation we have before us. Given the worldview that has likely been handed down to us, we cannot be blamed for wanting to change our child to fit "a mold" that we believe will make life easier for them. But what if instead of focusing on changing our child, we focused on the kind of parent we want to be?

These strategies are designed to create space for us to look inward and consider how we want to be present for and respond to our child, and help us be good to ourselves so we can show up for our child. Pick and choose what works for you, or find your own. The point is doing the work and finding the strategies and supports necessary to calibrate your nervous system so that you can live out the rest of the habits offered in this book.

Leverage biology

Calming our nervous system is as much biological as it is psychological. Use self-hugs, deep breathing, and meditation to reset.

It seems a bit silly at first, but your body doesn't know that. It just responds to the physical gesture of warmth and care, just as a baby responds to being held in its mother's arms. Remember, physical touch releases oxytocin, reduces cortisol, and calms cardiovascular stress (Dreisoerner *et al.* 2021).

So why not try it? If you notice that you're feeling tense, upset, or self-critical, try giving yourself a warm hug, or tenderly stroking your arm or face, or gently rocking your body. Research shows that what's important is that you make a clear gesture that conveys feelings of love, care, and tenderness. If other people are around, you can often fold your arms in a non-obvious way, gently squeezing yourself in a comforting manner. While you do so, notice how your body feels. Does it feel warmer, softer, calmer? It's amazing how easy it is to tap into our mammalian caregiving system to change our mood.

Get vulnerable

Let the mom or dad among us who has never made a mistake cast the first stone. But it is so hard to do when we are that parent. We are the grownup, we are supposed to know, right? Chances are we never heard our elders admit fault or even say "I am sorry" when we were growing up.

Social psychologist Brené Brown has led the charge in shaking up a righteous world (Brown 2022). There is hard research confirming the power of admitting our mistakes. The fact is we make mistakes all the time, and it is good for our kids to see us making them, particularly if we model using our mistakes as learning opportunities.

Your child is resilient, they can handle you making a mistake. An equally powerful benefit of vulnerability is that our child sees that the world does not vaporize when a mistake is made in the family and that we all recover and move on. Learning from your model, they will be less afraid of making mistakes themselves.

A good friend still cringes when she recounts how she consequenced her son's defiant behavior. "There he goes again zoning out, not listening and totally tuning us out," until she learned what she thought was defiance was active seizure behavior. She felt horrible once she realized, and she owned her mistake and her son was able to reconcile the error and move on.

LET'S GET VULNERABLE

Recall one of your least proud parenting moments (aka something you see now as a mistake or a misstep).

- How did your child react?
- What was the impact in the short run?
- What was the outcome in the long run?

Let go of "shoulds"

Anyone who has gotten trapped in an Instagram doom scroll featuring images of friends' perfect lives, or who dreads bringing in the mail for fear of opening one more idyllic family holiday card, knows the discontent of comparison. We know measuring ourselves up against others breeds discontent and, in extreme cases, self-hatred—yet we still fall prey. As parents of children with disabilities we are met daily with the contrasts between our own lives and those of our friends and neighbors who exist in neurotypical land—blissfully unaware that schools not accepting a child, treatments not being available, or a child being denied daycare or preschool because they don't meet the criteria are even "things."

It is high time for us to identify and shake off our own personal "shoulds." We unconsciously receive countless messages from the media, friends, and our own upbringing about what the experience of being a parent should be like. "I *should* be able to fix dinner while my daughter works quietly on her homework in her room." "I *should* be able to wave a cheery goodbye to my son as he independently boards the school bus." "I *should* be able to get myself ready for work in the morning as my child manages his own shower, dresses, and gets his backpack ready for school." "I *should* be able to enjoy watching my child participate in their favorite sport while I snap pictures from the sidelines." "I *should* be able to drop my kid off at birthday parties with a present in hand and use my free time to run errands." "I *should* be able to expect that my child will go to school dances, participate in extracurricular activities, take care of their younger siblings, find a job when they are 16, get a driver's license, and find an apartment just like I did when I was a kid." Should, should, should...and the list drones on.

Above all, get clear on two universal truths:

1. *This is not the parenting journey you imagined.* Admit to yourself, your partner, or a trusted friend that you did not "sign on" for the parenting journey on which you find yourself. Even those of us who had advance information because of in utero testing, or because they chose a child with challenges through adoption, still could not predict their day-to-day reality until they began living it. Owning this fact, this helps free ourselves from tired and outdated fallacies like "we are saints," "this is somehow our vocation in life," "we must be special people," or "we somehow willed or deserve a child with disability." Parents of children who think, move, behave, or communicate differently are not god-like. We are regular, fallible humans like everyone else. We have a right to get frustrated, wish things were easier, and yes, even to say "this sucks" once in a while.

2. *Normal is an illusion.* Capable parents realize that in a country

where one in five children identify as neurodivergent, whether diagnosed or not, "normal" is not a thing, and since it is an illusion, "normal" should not be the standard, but instead maybe a happy, rewarding, or meaningful life. In fact all of our families sit astride an ever shifting teeter totter of circumstance. Parenting comes with all kinds of difficult life situations, such as blended families, divorce, fostering, grandparents as parents, mental illness, anxiety and illness, deaths, emotional challenges, and economic uncertainties that expose "normal" as fallacy. The idyllic image of a two-parent hetero family with a stay-at-home mom meeting the kids at the door with cookies is nothing more than a black-and-white TV fantasy.

Once we settle the score with ourselves on these two facts, we are ready to let go of the shoulds that peek out of the dark corners of our minds to haunt us and truly enjoy the parenting life we do have.

SHAKE OFF SHOULDS

1. List the things you had imagined parents should do.

2. Now identify up to three beautiful, proud, or positive moments in your *real* parenting life.

These are part of your unique parenting experience. Celebrate and cherish them. Meanwhile, if it helps, tear up or even burn your shoulds list. Create new stories for yourself that revolve around your real parenting experience.

Say bye-bye to shame

We have enough to do raising our child so that they realize their best life, despite the challenges they face. We have no time to be bogged down by toxic or unhelpful emotions. Shame is a leader among these. While accepting guilt (when appropriate) and responsibility is important in developing a moral compass, feeling shame is almost always destructive. Shame can fool us into feeling bad about circumstances we have no control over. It can make us feel like bad parents, and cause us to be defensive and withdraw from others.

Parents of kids with disabilities are met with potentially shame-inducing situations on the daily. We are "ashamed" when our child behaves in ways outside age-specific accepted norms. We are ashamed of ourselves when we allow ourselves to be triggered by our child's behavior. We feel shame when we have to parent in ways others might not understand to help our child. We feel shame when we misread our child's cues and respond in inappropriate ways—after all we are the parent, we should have known.

Oftentimes shame is induced by the judgments or perceived judgments of others. They can come from trusted family members or professionals, complete strangers, or from the circumstances in which we find ourselves. Family members unwittingly made me feel bad that I was not letting my kid watch TV. Friends made me feel like I was being "harsh" by having my child carry picnic gear given his physical challenges. In each of these cases I knew what my child needed to thrive, and that was less time inert in front of a screen and repeated opportunities to engage in weight-bearing exercise. Then there was the therapist who made me ashamed of my child's oral fixation by proposing a solution that would single him out at school. Shoppers made me shrink because I could not "make" my eight-year-old stop talking in a baby-talk voice. Again I knew what was best for my child. Public embarrassment would not erase a serious sensory lag, and the baby-talk was actually Jack's own DIY strategy for increasing fluency and avoiding something that was more painful for him, stuttering.

If your child thinks, moves, communicates, or behaves differently, you likely can remember people or situations that have made you feel bad about what you knew was best for your child.

Capable parents are loving, intentional, and humble. They are intentional in weighing options, services, and supports for and with their child, given the vision of capable they have forged for and with their child. At the same time they recognize that they cannot possibly know everything, but they know that parenting is more an art than a science.

They accept that their parenting journey will be paved with mistakes. Above all, their intentions are governed by love, the goal of which is strengthening their connection with their child. Because their vision of capable provides a North Star, they maintain a degree of confidence in their parenting decisions. This allows them to let go of the shame-inducing judgments of others.

Anyone can have a bad day, and we do well to give others the grace that we would like shown to us. But if certain people or circumstances regularly make you feel bad about what you know to be intentional, loving parenting, let go of them. Don't go on picnics with those friends, find a new therapist, don't go to grandma's around TV time, or allow your child to listen to an audible book while at the store. If a family member feels they know better and refuses to follow the behavior rules in your home, you can choose to not have that person in a position where they are responsible for caring for your child.

This does not mean you need to let go of these people, places, or situations forever. Circumstances will change. You signed on to be a parent, not a human punchbag. The point is it is okay and even healthy to allow yourself to remove shame-inducing events and people from your orbit.

SAY BYE-BYE TO SHAME

Identify people and situations that are shame-inducing—and let go of them.

Be intentional about knowing when something is not good for you or your child. Take a break from those situations, places, or people. Nothing is forever—there may be a time to return but you and your child decide when that is.

The first step is to identify these people and situations:

- Are there places and situations that make you feel bad about your parenting?

- Are there specific people in these places or situations whose judgments are not welcome?

- If these people are family members who you don't or can't let go of, isolate the events or times that are the problem (their homes, evenings, overnights, or meals, etc.). Find ways to be with these family members outside of these situations.

- Remember, taking time away does not have to be forever; as circumstances change you can reintroduce yourself and your child.

View today's drama or trauma as temporary

When we are smack dab in the middle of a particularly tough time with our child, it is easy to catastrophize. My child went through a period of time where he kept the ends of two fingers lodged just inside his mouth with his hand trailing down his chin. Later there was a time when he responded to virtually every question using baby-talk. There were other behaviors like these, and when we were living through them with Jack, it seemed like they would be with us forever.

Perhaps you are experiencing behaviors that go well beyond those that merely discourage friendships and potentially "turn off" kids at school or on the playground. There are those of us whose child is throwing feces or who is actively hurting himself or others. And there are others whose child is refusing to leave her room or interact with the family. Regardless of mindset, these behaviors are difficult to endure.

When we are living with our child through such behaviors it can feel like time is standing still. We catastrophize and the thoughts surface like: "What if my child continues doing _____ [fill in the blank] forever?" "What if this behavior keeps her from school, friends, community placements?" and so on. When we dig deep we find catastrophizing is just another way to nurse a fixed mindset.

We rationally know that all behavior is communication and it doesn't matter that a specialist can find sensory, nervous system, environmental, or trauma explanations for them. We are living with our child day-to-day and what we see is troubling, heart-rending, and mystifying.

Of course we seek help for our child. In Jack's case help involved a particularly intuitive occupational therapist with sensory integration expertise and multiple speech therapists who understood the mysteries surrounding stuttering. But there is something else really important that capable parents do. We maintain a growth mindset and recognize that the current situation is not fixed but temporary, a short-term setback. We take the advice of parents who have come before us. We realize that today's drama or trauma, no matter how difficult, will not be forever.

This is not to say that serious behaviors are to be minimized as mere childhood phases. But it is true that whether neurodivergent or neurotypical our children's behavior changes. Think about your neurotypical child or even yourself when you were a child. Children go through periods when they are afraid of the dark, wet the bed, or insist on putting on the same outfit every morning. In almost all cases, those behaviors, no matter how disruptive at the time, have changed. They are not just gone, but other behaviors have taken their place.

The same is true of our neurodivergent children with troubling behaviors. You gain perspective that brings a degree of peace and are able to respond more positively to your child when you remember that behaviors are not fixed entities. Today's concern will likely be replaced with another one, but it will not last forever.

VIEW TODAY'S DRAMA OR TRAUMA AS TEMPORARY

1. Identify the current troubling behavior, trauma, or drama.

2. Put the current situation in perspective by recalling a behavior that your child has exhibited in the past.

   - How did the past behavior resolve?

   - Does the behavior still persist?

   - How did it change?

3. What factors helped it resolve?

4. Looking back, how long did it last? (Likely not forever.)

5. Reflect on how you feel when you view behaviors as not permanent but time-limited.

Now imagine a resolution to the current trauma or drama.

Out yourself

Raising a child who is neurodivergent or who has a disability in a "neurotypical" world can be a lonely existence. We are bombarded with families around us having what to us look to be typical, enjoyable experiences—watching their kids' football game, cheering at competitions, talking about boyfriends or girlfriends, taking their kid trick-or-treating, dropping them off for sleepovers at friends' houses, or going with them to choose a prom dress or to get a driver's license.

We know that each of these may be fraught with their own angst, but to the extent they differ from our own experience, they look like nirvana. Meanwhile, it feels like we are stuck in one gear, just shuttling our child from one therapy or IEP meeting to the next.

The greater the experience of people in our orbits diverges from our own the more we are likely to retreat and hide. We clam up around parents who are sharing their child's (seemingly) carefree, exciting antics and wait it out at neighborhood gatherings until mercifully someone has to leave or the subject changes. I remember enduring in silence through a tight-lipped smile three moms' excited chatter about the challenge of getting a restaurant reservation for their sons' large prom contingent of friends. All the while, I muzzled the challenge that was weighing on my mind: How I was going to spend the time with my son when he was not included in a single group for that magical high school rite of passage.

We each have our own comfort level and know our own setpoint for privacy. You choose when or what to share, but recognize that when you do share your experience it lightens your load. When you break your silence, you may find an ally you didn't know you had or that other people's kids, even the "neurotypies," are struggling in similar ways.

A side benefit is that your sharing provides a learning opportunity for others and a connection. Because even if their child's issues are different they still are witnessing their child struggle, and that is the great leveler for all of us parents the world around.

When I finally broke my silence and shared that my child struggled making even the simplest decisions, my friend offered me a "me too" knowing glance and shared that her son (who happened to be on the honor roll) was forgetting his homework and questioning himself on what he should wear to school to the point of missing the bus. "I swear it feels like when they turn 14 they go back to the emotional intelligence of a four-year-old," she said. We both were able to share a laugh. The effect of putting my own concern out there was relief and connection.

Sharing and listening to another person's story taught me that perhaps my son's "executive functioning delays" were not so wildly different from the decision-making difficulties that other adolescents were going through. I was reminded of the fact that development across all kids is uneven, and confidence falters—it was just that my child's difficulties came with a formal label. Together we learned that we had a worry in common—how to help our children organize their thinking, gain confidence, and learn to trust their decisions.

OUT YOURSELF

- Identify a trusted person.

- Share with them a challenge you are having parenting your child.

- Listen to their response.

- What is similar or dissimilar in their experience?

A side benefit is the learning opportunity that it provides for other parents, particularly parents of neurotypical children.

- Think of a time you have shared with a friend.

  – What did you share?

  – What was the other person's response?

  – What did you learn?

Find and commit to your own form of self-care

There are volumes written on the benefits of taking time out for ourselves. Every caregiver needs to take seriously the task of taking care of themself. This is true whether we are caught up in the rigors of parenting in general, caring for our own aging parents, or caring for a friend with cancer. Even the experts disagree about scope and types of self-care. Some cite up to eight types including physical, psychological, emotional, social, professional, environmental, spiritual, and even financial. While no doubt each of these is valuable to being a healthy individual, I am the kind of person who becomes anxious just seeing a list like this—my eyes glaze over thinking self-care is yet another area where I am falling behind.

That is why I like life coach and author of *Differently Wired* Debbie Reber's simple definition of self-care as daily actions that are (1) intentional and (2) just for you (Reber 2020). Now that is a definition that most parents, even those of us who are totally overwhelmed and running on fumes, can get behind. According to Debbie's definition, self-care is not just those popular elixirs that social media tries to sell us on, like pilates, meditation, goat yoga, running, or reading the classics. It can be anything you choose to do that works for you, as standard or quirky as you please. If dancing in your living room, tending herbs, making sourdough, eating cheese, swaying in your hammock, playing with your dog, organizing your spice rack, lifting weights, or zoning out to an episode of *Friends* works for you, so be it. It qualifies as long as it is just for you. And here is the best part: According to Reber, your child can even be with you as long as you are calling the shots and engaging in the activity on your terms.

However, when our child has a disability and requires round-the-clock care, it can be difficult to isolate that time. Just like with buying a house or getting pregnant, if you wait for the perfect time you will never do it. So find an imperfect time, 20 minutes at least (depending on the activity, maybe an hour or longer), and commit to taking that time, every day if possible, but at least three times a week. Regardless of whether our child wants our attention or the world is on fire, we escape to our intentional, just-for-us activity for that time.

Change your mindset by changing the language you use around your chosen self-care. Don't apologize to yourself or others by saying "I am sorry but I need to _____" or "I wish I didn't have to _____." Don't act like taking time for yourself is a chore by saying things like "I would like to take time for _____" or "I hope I get to _____ today." Use declarative language that tells you and everyone else that you value your self-care and do not compromise when it comes to it. "I don't miss my yoga, time in my hammock, my cup of tea with a book, my adult coloring time [or whatever it is]." Research on exercise has shown that people who refer to their workout with imperative language are more likely to maintain their routine over time.

FIND AND COMMIT TO YOUR OWN FORM OF SELF-CARE

Recharging our batteries in order to show up for our child day in and day out is not optional.

1. Find your own form of self-care that is intentional and just for you.

2. Identify a time and commit to practicing it for at least 20 minutes three times a week.

3. Change your mindset around self-care by talking about your activity using declarative language: "I never miss _____."

4. Tell a friend so you have an "accountability partner" checking in with you.

Identify and use trusted helpers

Nothing draws out our mama or papa bear claws like a wounded cub. When our child is more likely to be misunderstood, misjudged, or taken advantage of due to neurodivergence or disability, our tendency is to protect. Because of my son's communication difficulties there was a time that I always felt I had to be on hand to finish a sentence, bridge a conversation, or fill in context to clarify a thought. It had become such a habit that I don't even think I recognized that I was doing it.

Of course, no one loves and cares for our child like we do, and we value consistency. But the more we do for our child the more they become accustomed to us being there, and the more we think we are the only ones who can do what we do. Another self-fulfilling prophecy.

When we try to be everything for our child, not only do we burn ourselves out, but we rob our child of valuable relationships and enriching experiences. We fear that no one can do our job. More than a few parents I have worked with have shared that they are afraid that they will die and no one will take care of their child like they do.

Snow's (1998) circles of support provides an invaluable model for thinking about the people in our child's life and expanding their networks. Her work has identified four concentric circles beginning with the immediate family (mom, dad, brothers, sisters) in the center and fanning out to friendships (people with whom your child spends leisure time), participation (people with which your child engages in shared interests), and exchange (therapists, doctors, aides, and other paid relationships your child has). Usually our children with disabilities have a comparable number of people in their inner circle of immediate family members, as do neurotypical kids. However, when it comes to friendships, actual people they can contact to engage in fun and leisure activities, the number dwindles with too many children having none.

Look at all the activities, therapies, training, and events you do with your child on a weekly basis. Consider the areas where you can let go and let others do for your child. Reflect on why you haven't let go of any of these to date. Break through your resistance to asking for help. Remember your child has much to gain from building relationships with people other than you.

Just like parents the world over we often feel like glorified chauffeurs for our kids. Often if our kid has extraordinary medical needs, assistive technology, or concerning behaviors we are less likely to trust them to a car pool. If there are no safety concerns that necessitate your presence, consider partnering up with another parent or small group of parents to lighten your load—particularly as it relates to getting your child to and from school. If you also have neurotypical kids, no doubt they regularly drive with other parents. Your child will gain skills and flexibility by having to get used to a new driver, new situations, and new rules, and bonus, they may even make new friends.

Identify another trusted adult who would like to take your child to one therapy or activity a week. As much as we love to be there and get progress updates in person, routine texts and emails can provide you with the same information.

Find and train babysitters, caregivers, or companions who can give you a break. Pay them to shadow you so they know your expectations for your child (see Habit #7).

IDENTIFY AND USE TRUSTED HELPERS

Recognize that you don't need to be and can't be everything for your child. In fact it is not desirable. Your child has more to gain building relationships with others than he has to lose from the consistency that will be lost between you and the trusted caregiver. You can't be everything for your child.

1. Make a list of all the activities, therapies, training, and events you do with your child on a weekly basis.

2. Consider areas where you could identify a trusted helper to take over.

3. Reflect on why you haven't let go of any of these to date.

4. Break through your resistance to asking for help.

5. See how your child responds to the new relationships.

Epilogue: Affiliation, Friendship, and Relationships

In my first book, *Capable*, I share my story of raising Jack. It is singular and quirky, heart-rending, and inspiring. It is as unique to our family as your story is to yours. But writing this book was a whole different animal. Although it was me who captured words on paper, *Raising Capable Kids* is not mine, it is *our* story. It is for all of us—the moms and dads, grandmas and grandpas, aunties and uncles, and foster parents who are loving, supporting, and challenging their neurodivergent child day in and day out.

I chose to introduce each chapter with a compelling real-life tale in hopes of "hooking" readers on the Habit that followed. I am confident that when you adopt the Habits offered in the 12 preceding chapters you will exponentially increase your chances of raising a kid who feels seen, knows himself, and who has what it takes to meet the challenges that life holds for him. This is true whether your child's particular challenge looks like sharing their voice with the world using a communication device, calming their nervous system just enough to break a routine and try something new, persevering through a page of math problems when distractions feel insurmountable, or showing up with the confidence to land a job that matches their passion.

Still, with all that neuroscience has to say about what we can do to build agency within our kids, help them feel safe enough to take the risks necessary to learn, and how to foster a strong sense of self, parenting remains risky business, an inexact science. I laughed out loud when I recently read Bonnie Garmus's musings about parenting in *Lessons in Chemistry* (2022): "Yet here she was…a mother, the lead scientist on what had to be the most unscientific experiment ever: the raising of another human being." Even with our best efforts, and knowledge of the neuroscience behind parenting, personal motivation, free will, context, and an incalculable tangle of individual differences ensure that parenting is not a straightforward in-and-out equation. But then we knew this when we signed up for the hardest job we'd ever love.

Parents, despite this all-caps, no-guarantees disclaimer, it is still critical that you adopt the Habits. I made them my own because I wanted to make sure I left nothing on the table in giving my son the best chance I could in a world that is all too ready to dismiss their fellow human beings based on how they look, move, or speak. My missteps were many, but on balance I tried to mindfully live out the Habits. Still I am thoughtful about behaving and speaking in ways that increase self-knowledge, build a narrative of strength, and challenge my son with support. Even today I try to offer extra doses of each of these, believing that it is never too late to make a difference with your kid.

One thing I have learned over time is that there is an area which no amount of parental support will "fix," and that is making friendships. Lasting friendships are governed by an idiosyncratic web of variables that defy pat formulas. We only have to reflect on our own close relationships to know that this is true. But what intentionally practicing capable parenting habits did was help me teach my son to follow his special interests, encourage the resilience needed for him to continue putting himself out there over and over again, and help him feel safe enough to be curious about and take a sincere interest in others. Even allowing for neurodivergence, these are all the ingredients that leading relationship researchers have found to increase the odds that real friendships will form (Franco 2022).

Ironically, as I was typing these final paragraphs, my stream of consciousness was broken by a call from my eldest son. Now a young man of 25, Jack has a job that he loves and lives in the city in an apartment that he shares with a roommate. He searches online for MeetUp groups that connect him with others who share his love of long-distance running, volleyball, sci-fi writing, and all things Stephen King. He is busy living life on his own terms and sometimes forgets to call his mom. But on this day he did not, and the smile I feel in his voice creates a glow within me that I know will last long after we hang up.

Sure, undefined challenges lie ahead just below the surface with their disappointments and heartaches like silent emotional land-mines. This is true for all of us whether we were labeled "different" as a child or not. But it is nothing like when he was little, and we were met with angst-producing unknowns lurking around every corner. What is wrong? Will he fit in? Will he be judged? Will he be turned away? Can I take it if he is rejected again? Does an appropriate therapy exist, and how do we pay for it? What will happen when that teacher that "gets him" leaves?

Those old fears only exist now as dull memories. My heart is still, safe in the knowledge that Jack has the tools to face whatever trials present themselves. And even more than that, I know with certainty that the same world which conspired to sort, judge, and dismiss Jack is today a better place for him being in it. What more could a mother want?

APPENDICES

CAPABLE PARENTING HABIT GUIDES

CAPABLE PARENTING

Habit #1 Capable Parents believe that effort creates ability.

Date:

My Notes:

Key Ideas:
- Potential is not fixed—effort can trump diagnostic predictions.
- "Effort" may require different or additional supports and scaffolds.
- This belief guides all decisions you make with and on behalf of your child.
- Don't allow the formality or finality of the diagnosis to cause you to question this fundamental belief for your child.
- We are not talking about "curing" our child, because that implies that our child is the problem, rather we are focused on enabling our child to live their best life—regardless of the challenges they face.

This habit is made up of two parts:
- We believe that we and our children improve through effort, not raw ability.
- This belief gives way to thoughts, decisions, and behaviors that provide our child with limitless opportunities to change and grow.

  Beliefs lead to **decisions** that prompt **behaviors** which provide
  opportunities for change and growth that **etch new neural pathways**.

  Consider the Power of B²: Beliefs and behavior working together

Try it on...
Follow the B² formula to identify growth opportunities for your child.
Consider:
One **belief** about your child's potential: (I believe that my child may someday...walk, use their communication device to participate in family parties, text people as a way to communicate, cross the street independently, use their bike to navigate their community, take notes in a college course, etc.)
_____

List:
thoughts that support that belief_____
decisions that could flow from that belief _____
behaviors that could follow _____
opportunities for growth_____

CAPABLE PARENTING

Habit #2 Capable Parents listen to their child and lean in to their natural curiosities to build agency, develop skills, and have fun.

Date:

My Notes:

Key Ideas:
- Listen (really listen) to your child and pay attention to behavioral cues that signal what makes your child happy or proud.
- Much of the progress that your child has made up until now has occurred thanks to natural curiosity.
- Take care not to confuse what YOU think will make your child happy or proud with what authentically makes them happy.
- You can "mine" pieces of an intense or unusual interest to help your child build skills and social connections.
- You can help them maintain their interest in appropriate ways.
- You can help your child find his people or places—other kids or contexts where the interest is shared.
- Interests wax and wane; when you are in the thick of it, it may seem like forever, but the fact is what your child is passionate about will change over time.

Try it on...
Determine the function of an intense interest or passion. Lean in to encourage new learning or appropriate ways to maintain the interest.

Carefully observe your child engaged in an intense interest or passion.

Determine the function of that interest/passion.

Is it...
- soothing?
- nervous system regulating?
- competence or confidence building?

Does it...
- hurt themself or others?
- get in the way of learning new skills, connecting with others, engaging in important daily routines?
- significantly disrupt others?

Use this information to determine how you want to lean in to support the interest, encourage them to pursue the interest in positive ways, or even how to leverage their natural curiosity to help them expand the interest, learn new skills, work on deficit areas, or take on a new challenge.

CAPABLE PARENTING

Habit #3 Capable Parents set a Vision of Capable with their child and adjust it as necessary.

Date:

My Notes:

Key Ideas:
- A Vision of Capable is a shared belief about your child's future which is informed and shaped by their interests, motivations, and passions, and by your hopes for them.
- In order to create a realistic Vision parents have to have clarity about "the present" as well as "the possible." It is important to imagine the possible for your child... while being honest about the present (or current state).
- To move toward the Vision, it is helpful to focus on the "next 15 yards"—identify the next step for your child and create opportunities for them to make those yards.

An effective Vision of Capable:

- acknowledges the present while using what you know about your child to signal "the possible"
- is rooted in your child's interests, skills, and passions
- is informed by what you know about your child
- is revised over time
- is used as the "litmus test" when considering accommodations, modifications, and services that come your child's way.

Try it on:
Craft a vision of capable for/with your child:

What is possible...

What is now...

⟶

Informed by:
Your child's interests, passions, natural curiosities, skills, and what you know about your child.

The "next 15 yards"
Identify a doable next step for your child:

CAPABLE PARENTING

Habit #4 Capable Parents put the diagnosis in its place, your child is a kid first.

Date:

My Notes:

Key Ideas:
- Stages of accepting the diagnosis—Disbelief, Denial, Anger, Assimilation.
- The diagnosis is all about Information, Information, Information, but does not define your child.
- Use it for the supports it can get your child.
- Avoid confirmation bias. Take care to not get caught up expecting to see or looking for the characteristics of your child's diagnosis because it will shape your beliefs about what your kid can do.
- Be intentional about when and how to talk with your child about their diagnosis.
- Use words that describe your child's strengths and frame challenges as opportunities for growth.

Reflection Questions
- What words do you use with your child to talk about their diagnosis?
- How do you frame your child's strengths and challenges?
- How does your child respond to information about their diagnosis?
- How does how you talk about your child's strengths/challenges/diagnosis align with their identity/view of themselves?

Try it on: Use all the words you would use to describe your child to create a "whole child" picture. Reflect on where their diagnosis fits in.

Created by Deborah Winking using www.wordclouds.com

CAPABLE PARENTING

> **Habit #5** Capable Parents name their fears and tame them in light of their Vision of Capable.

Date:

My Notes:

Key Ideas:

- Instead of hyperfocusing on changing your child, focus on the parent you want to be.
- Fear is hard-wired in us, as parents. It is a protective response as old as the cavemen.
- All parents worry, but there is even greater intensity to our fears when our child is apt to be prejudged by how they look, move, communicate, think, or behave.
- Evolution has wired us to react to fear through fleeing, fighting, or freezing. Our brains literally will not let us carefully process alternatives when we are fearful, that is why we need to tame our fears in order do our best job parenting.

An Incomplete List of Parenting Fears:

- Nothing is how it is supposed to be.
- My child, I won't fit in.
- My child will be made fun of, passed over.
- My child will be ostracized, rejected.
- My child will be lonely.
- I will not be able to access or pay for the therapies needed.
- I will be embarrassed.
- I am not doing enough.
- There is a new therapy I am neglecting.
- I am engaging my child in too many therapies and not letting him just be a kid.
- What if services at the next level or the next place are not good?
- I am pushing too hard.
- I am not pushing hard enough.
- My child will miss out on opportunities.
- Others in the family will be neglected as we prioritize one child's needs.
- Where will my child go, what will he do when I am no longer around?

Try it on: Tame that fear by examining it against the Vision of Capable you built with your child.

1. **Get clear about one fear.** Name it out loud. Notice what happens in your body when you put it into words.

2. **Acknowledge past reaction.** How have you reacted in the past when you are met with this fear?

3. **Calm.** Once you have named your fear, you are able to calm your nervous system and think clearly. You can now consider your fear through the lens of the Vision of Capable you have created with your child.

4. **Revisit the Vision of Capable.** Ask yourself: What could happen if that vision is realized? How does this fear potentially impact the vision?

5. **Use the Vision to put your fear into perspective.** Committing to your Vision will help you manage your fear.

CAPABLE PARENTING

Habit #6 Capable Parents use words and act in ways that send their child the message that they think their child is capable.

Date:

My Notes:

Key Ideas:
- It is not only the words we use and what we do but also what we don't say and do that send our child messages.
- Because it is harder to undo negative messages, err on the side of letting your child know that you believe "they can" even sometimes before you are 100% sure.
- It is through these messages that what you BELIEVE your child can do actually impacts your child's performance over time.

Reflection Questions
- How do I communicate to my child that I believe they are capable?
- What specific words and/or actions do I use? What messages do I send that communicate otherwise?
- What is my Vision with and for my child?
- Think about the decisions, small and large, along the way that support that Vision and the words and actions that support those decisions.
- How might I change the messages I send my child?

Try it on:
Use a journal or your phone to track your interactions for a couple of weeks. Note the things you say to your child (including those that you say within earshot of your child) as well as the way you behave toward your child. Note the things you don't say to your child and the things in which you don't include them. If you have a partner, review each other's journals. Review your journal(s) in light of the questions above.

CAPABLE PARENTING

Habit #7 Capable Parents set the expectation that others treat their child as capable.

Date:

My Notes:

Key Ideas:

- Helpers, do-gooders, and "well-meaners" do more harm than good over time, if they are allowed to send your child the message that they are not capable.
- Learned helplessness is not acting, or limiting your actions, because you have come to believe that you can't do something or that whatever you do will not make a difference.
- There are three classes of people your child encounters every day: Strangers, Regular Interactors, and the Pros.
- Strangers:
  - They are ubiquitous and largely out of your control.
  - Use a polite "He's got this" that turns into an "I've got this" over time.
- Regular Interactors
  - Bus drivers, cafeteria staff, other parents.
  - Show them—let them know that you want them to take their cues from you.
- The Pros
  - Teachers, aides, therapists, doctors.
  - Communicate your expectations clearly; share your Vision of Capable and get it put into the IEP.

Reflection Questions

- What are caregivers doing for your child?
- What personal care, academic, and/or physical tasks does your child legitimately need support and/or accommodations to complete?
- Are there pieces of these tasks that your child may be able to accomplish?
- How can support be decreased over time?

Try it on:

Practice "showing" or modeling for others the expectations you have for your child. Write or dictate into your phone a short statement of your Vision of Capable for your child. Share that Vision with the professionals who work with your child. Get the Vision written into the IEP. Work with professionals to get goals for phasing out support. Observe how your child responds as support is faded. What happens over time to your child's need for help?

CAPABLE PARENTING

Habit #8 Capable Parents challenge their child (in safe ways) that take their child and them out of their comfort zone to encourage growth.	**Date:**
	My Notes:

Key Ideas:

- The power of "safe" challenge: the amount of challenge that motivates and encourages as opposed to frustrates. It is the "just right" sweet spot of difficulty, the "Goldilocks zone" or zone of proximal development.
- Productive struggle: the process of effortful learning we engage in when we are faced with problems we don't immediately know how to solve.
- Allowing children to engage in productive struggle helps build and strengthen new neural pathways allowing them to master new skills over time.
- Three ways we help our child build new neural pathways are (1) asking them to supply answers or "show us" the next step rather than just identify it, (2) having them alternate practicing two or more new skills, instead of just practicing the same one, and (3) engaging them in brief practice opportunities spaced out over time—instead of longer practice opportunities.
- Challenge encourages growth, but comfort has its place when your child is dysregulated or when their nervous system is overtaxed. Other conditions like autistic burnout call for reduced demands, while supporting and "gently" encouraging your child.

Reflection Questions

- Do you give your child time and support to engage in problems and challenges that are not immediately solvable?
- Where are you prioritizing comfort over challenge for your child?
- How do time constraints and schedule concerns get in the way?
- What are you allowing your child to opt out of?
- What are you fearful about your child doing/trying/being?
- How do you teach your child to welcome "challenge" in their life?

Try it on:

Use a journal or your phone to reflect on where you are prioritizing comfort over challenge for your child. Think about why you are choosing comfort. Identify one specific area where your child would benefit from challenge. What would it take to engage your child in productive struggle in that area? Could you use one of the three strategies above to help your child build new neural pathways?

Revisit your shared Vision of Capable. Reflect on the trade-offs of choosing comfort over challenge for your child. For you?

CAPABLE PARENTING

> **Habit #9** Capable Parents walk alongside professionals to get their child the support and services that they need.

> **Date:**

> **Try DIY Therapy—**
> Therapies are critical, but the time in structured therapy alone is usually not enough for your child to make lasting gains. Capable Parents find opportunities throughout the day to practice therapy goals as a part of "doing life" together.

Key Ideas:
- Capable Parents recognize that they know their child better than anyone.
- They use their knowledge of how their child best (1) learns, (2) communicates, and (3) relates to others to get their child what they need to succeed.
- They keep their Vision of Capable (Habit #3) front and center and use it to judge the desirability of the supports, accommodations, and modifications that are offered to their child.
- They help their child build the self-knowledge necessary to take advantage of learning opportunities and advocate for the supports and services that help them thrive.
- Capable Parents are clear about their Vision of Capable and desired outcomes: "the what" they want for their child. They hold firm on "the what" but are willing to consider creative alternatives on "how" to get to the Vision.

"Walking Alongside" Steps
1. **Observe your child's learning and behavior.** Find the situations and people that are challenging and comforting for your child.

2. **Talk with your child about what works for them.** Ask questions and communicate with your child about what feels good when they are learning, helps them focus, and makes them want to learn and spend time with others.

3. **Clearly communicate the Vision of Capable to the team.** Share with the team the Vision of Capable you hold with your child.

4. **Agree on desired outcome(s) with the team.** Come to agreement on the desired outcomes of services with the IEP team. Ensure that the desired outcome is written into the IEP.

5. **Consider alternatives that meet the desired outcome.** Listen to the team, paraphrase possible concerns, and be open to creative ways to meet the desired outcome.

6. **Agree on a plan.** Agree on a plan to meet desired outcomes, check in, and be prepared to revise the plan as necessary.

Try it on:
Create a DIY therapy. Identify the goal(s) of one therapy your child receives (e.g., occupational therapy, physiotherapy, speech therapy, etc.). Find or create one way to practice a therapy goal or goals in the regular course of "doing life" every day with your child. Practice your DIY therapy regularly to exponentially increase the benefits of therapy for your child.

CAPABLE PARENTING

Habit #10 Capable Parents allow their child to make choices and experience the consequences of those choices.

Date:

My Notes:

Key Ideas:

- Good decision-makers are not born...they are made.
- In general, society provides "neurotypical" kids with practice in making choices and experiencing consequences through the regular course of growing up. Too often this process gets short-circuited for kids with disabilities.
- Offer your child "what," "when," "who," and "where" choices to help them to build skills, agency, and self-knowledge.
- Help your child reflect on choices they have made. Ask them what they liked and didn't like, how they felt after they made their choice, and what surprised them.

Consequences Clarified

Consequences come in two flavors: positive and negative. They can be natural or imposed. Natural consequences are the best (but only work when they matter to your child). Intention is key with imposed consequences. If you are angry, frustrated, or dysregulated, your child will get the message that "adults can cause me pain by taking things away from me." If you lead with love and concern, your child gets the message that you are concerned and want them to be successful.

Your child can sense your intention in imposing the consequence.

Examples: Imposed Consequence

Leading with anger and frustration: "That is it, I am taking your Furby because you have been turning in blank math pages."

Leading with love and concern: "The blank math page makes me think you need more help to focus. I am worried that the Furby is taking all your attention, so let's find a place to put it until you are done."

Reflect:

1. How do you regularly help your child flex their decision-making muscles?
2. In what situations do you let your child experience the consequences of their actions? Are there times when you intervene?
3. What kinds of choices do you allow/encourage your child to make?
4. What kinds of choices do you make for your child?

Try it on:

1. Help your child flex their choice-making muscles. Offer them a choice. After they have made the choice and experienced its result, spend some time asking them questions. Did they like the result of their choice? What surprised them? What would they do differently next time if they had to make the decision again? What else can you do to get them to think more about their choices?

2. Think of a time when your child encountered a limit or experienced a consequence as a result of their choices or behavior. Did you allow them to experience the consequence or did you intervene? How did your child react? What would you do the same or differently next time?

CAPABLE PARENTING

CAPABLE PARENTING

> **Habit #11** Capable Parents celebrate their child's persistence to help them build a narrative of strength.

> **Date:**
>
> **My Notes:**

Key Ideas:

- Experts estimate that, by age 10, kids experiencing ADHD receive 20,000 more negative comments than they have positive ones. Kids with ASD and other disabilities have lower self-worth than kids without.
- Experiences are logged as "wins" or "losses" and can become part of a child's personal narrative.
- Parents can shift that balance by calling out their child's hard work, persistence, resilience, and determination rather than focusing on the details of what their kid gets "right or wrong" or how "fast" they get it done.
- Meet your child where they are. This may mean noticing, calling out, and reinforcing behavior that approximates what you hope to see, beginning steps or even just approaching a new task. This is how desired behavior is shaped.

Tipping the Balance

When we actively "notice" and emphasize persistence, doing the right thing even when it is hard, curiosity, and trying new things, we teach our child that their brain is a learning machine that eats up challenges as its fuel. Staying safe and avoiding those things that at first blush seem difficult or demanding starves your child's brain. The message to your kid is "I can do hard things" and "persisting through trials is actually fun because it makes me better and stronger!"

Reflection Questions

1. What positive messages does your child regularly receive from their environment? What negative messages do they receive?
2. What can you do to help them mediate those messages?
3. How do you frame your child's successes?
4. How do you frame your child's struggles?
5. What is your focus when your child is learning something or having new experiences? Correctness or persistence? Process or precision?
6. How does your child react to disappointments or struggles?
7. How do you react when your child experiences disappointment or when they struggle?

Try it on:

1. Help your child develop their own narrative of strength. Intentionally call out and praise your child around "process" instead of "outcome." Choose one of the following: (1) their persistence at a task, (2) creative ideas or "outside the box" perspectives they contribute, (3) an unusual strategy they use to solve a problem, (4) the positive attitude they show, (5) how they encourage and cheer on others, or (6) their dogged pursuit of a solution even when it takes a long time. Call out and emphasize this quality with your child whenever you see it in action. Notice how your child reacts to new challenges in the future.

2. Put tests in their place. Any time a test is used with your child, make a point of asking exactly what inferences (conclusions) can fairly be made based on the measure. Ask this question: What skills and behaviors does this test measure and what does it not measure?

CAPABLE PARENTING

> **Habit #12** Treat yourself with compassion, make mistakes, laugh and learn from them.

Date:

My Notes:

Key Ideas:

- A #1 parenting fear is that we are not up for the job.
- Being afraid of making mistakes can immobilize us in unhelpful ways.
- Our kids are resilient.
- Model for your child that it is okay to make mistakes and that we all recover from them.
- Our kids need to see (and feel) that we take care of ourselves.

Paths to Self-Care

- **Get vulnerable**—Remind yourself and model for your child that we all recover from our mistakes. Recall one "least proud parenting moment," something you now consider a "mistake." How did your child respond at the time? What was the long-term impact?
- **Let go of "shoulds"**—Identify your ideas of what life as a mom or dad "should look like" and let go of them. "Normal" is an illusion. Instead identify two or three beautiful, proud, or positive moments in your REAL parenting life. Celebrate these!
- **Say goodbye to shame**—Identify people and situations that are shame-inducing, and let go of them. They will not help you on your journey.
- **Recognize and reject fixed mindsets**—Realize that today's drama or trauma, no matter how difficult, will not last forever. To prove this fact to yourself, identify something that used to be an issue for your child that no longer is a concern. New challenges will arise and current challenges will subside.
- **Out yourself**—Open up to another person about a parenting challenge that you are experiencing. It is a learning opportunity for others (particularly parents of neurotypical kids), and you will find commonalities with other parents that you never knew existed. You are not alone!
- **Create your own "brand" of self-care**—Commit to filling your empty tank. The only rule is that whatever you choose, it has to be exclusively FOR YOU. Allocate 15 minutes a day at least.
- **Identify and use reliable helpers**—You can't be, nor should you be, everything for your child. Identify one willing, trusted person and a role they might fill. Reach out to them. Break through your resistance to asking for help.
- **Parent in community**—Find a supportive group and stick with it.

Try it on:

Start out by choosing one path above. Take note of how committing to it makes you feel about your parenting, your child, and yourself.

Suggested Reading

I invite you to explore the resources that influenced my thinking and research around *Raising Capable Kids*.

Duckworth, A. (2018) *Grit: The Power of Passion and Perseverance*. New York, NY: Scribner.

Dweck, C.S. (2007) *Mindset: The New Psychology of Success*. New York, NY: Random House.

Forbes, H. (2009) *Dare to Love: The Art of Merging Science and Love into Parenting Children with Difficult Behaviors*. Boulder, CO: Beyond Consequences Institute.

Jackson, Y. (2011) *The Pedagogy of Confidence-Inspiring High Intellectual Performance in Urban Schools*. New York, NY: Teachers College Columbia University.

Jekanowski, E. (2021) *Learning and Living with Autism: A Story of Hope*. Hobe Sound, FL: Divina Press.

Jensen, E. (1998) *Teaching with the Brain in Mind*. Alexandria, VA: ASCD.

Moore, S. (2022) *Peaceful Discipline*. Saint Paul, MN: Pond Reads Press.

Pink, D.H. (2006) *A Whole New Mind—Why Right Brainer Will Rule the Future*. New York, NY: Riverhead Books.

Reber, D. (2019) *Differently Wired*. New York, NY: Workman Press.

Reeves, K. and Cunningham, R. (2018) *Raising Ryan: Living with Autism*. Bellingham, WA: TSK Adventures Press.

Shannon, S. and Heckman, E. (2007) *Please Don't Label My Child*. New York, NY: Rodale.

Siegel, DJ. and Bryson, T.P. (2012) *The Whole Brain Child*. New York, NY: Bantam Books.

Tough, P. (2012) *How Children Succeed: Grit, Curiosity, and Hidden Power of Character*. New York, NY: Houghton Mifflin.

Van Der Klift, E. and Kunc, N. (2019) *Being Realistic Isn't Realistic*. CA: Tellwell.

Winner, M.G. (2008) *Think Social: A Social Thinking Curriculum for School Aged Students*. San Jose, CA: Think Social Publishing.

References

Blaska, J.K. (1998) "Cyclical grieving: Reoccurring emotions experienced by parents who have children with disabilities." Available online at https://eric.ed.gov/?id=ED419349

Bogdanov, J. (2023) "How to help a child with ADHD at home with 1 powerful idea." Child Behavior Clinic. https://childbehaviorclinic.com/how-to-help-a-child-with-adhd-at-home-with-1-powerful-idea

Boo, K. (2014) *Behind the Beautiful Forevers: Life, Death, and Hope in a Mumbai Undercity.* New York, NY: Random House.

Brown, B. (2022) *The Gifts of Imperfection.* Center City, MN: Hazelden.

Childcare Education Institute (2021) "Confirmation bias and how it detracts from teachable moments." www.cceionline.com/confirmation-bias-and-how-it-detracts-from-teachable-moments

Clear, J. (2018) *Atomic Habits: An Easy & Proven Way to Build Good Habits & Break Bad Ones.* New York, NY: Avery, an imprint of Random House.

Cutler, E. (2016) *A Thorn in My Pocket.* Arlington, TX: Future Horizons, Inc.

Dreisoerner, A., Junker, N.M., Schlotz, W., Heimrich, J., *et al.* (2021) "Self-soothing touch and being hugged reduce cortisol responses to stress: A randomized controlled trial on stress, physical touch, and social identity." *Comprehensive Psychoneuroendocrinology 8*, 100091. doi:10.1016/j.cpnec.2021.100091

Duckworth, A. (2018) *Grit: The Power of Passion and Perseverance.* New York, NY: Scribner.

Dweck, C.S. (2007) *Mindset: The New Psychology of Success.* New York, NY: Random House.

Felitti, V.J., Anda, R.F., Nordenberg, D., Edwards, V., *et al.* (1998) "Relationship of childhood abuse and household dysfunction to many of the leading causes of death in adults: The Adverse Childhood Experiences (ACE) Study." *American Journal of Preventive Medicine 14*, 4, 245–258.

Fernald, A. (1993) "Approval and disapproval: Infant responsiveness to vocal affect in familiar and unfamiliar languages." *Child Development 64*, 3, 657–674.

Franco, M.G. (2022) *Platonic: How the Science of Attachment Can Help You Make—and Keep—Friends.* New York, NY: G.P. Putnam's Sons.

Garmus, B. (2022) *Lessons in Chemistry.* New York, NY: Doubleday.

Herrnstein, R. and Murray, C. (1994) *The Bell Curve: Intelligence and Class Structure in American Life*. New York, NY: Free Press.

Kidd, C. and Hayden, B.Y. (2015) "The psychology and neuroscience of curiosity." *Neuron 88*, 449–460.

May, K.T. (2015, March 17) "A walk with Daniel Kish, who navigates the world using 'flash sonar.'" https://ideas.ted.com/a-walk-with-daniel-kish-the-real-life-batman

McLean, K.C. (2005) "Late adolescent identity development: Narrative meaning making and memory telling." *Developmental Psychology 41*, 683–691.

Moore, S.R. (2022) *Peaceful Discipline: Story Teaching, Brain Science and Better Behavior*. Saint Paul, MN: Pond Reads Press.

National Institute for Children's Health Quality (n.d.) "Children's social and emotional development starts with co-regulation." https://nichq.org/insight/childrens-social-and-emotional-development-starts-co-regulation

Newman, L., Wagner, M., Knokey, A.-M., Marder, C., *et al.* (2011) *The Post-High School Outcomes of Young Adults with Disabilities up to 8 Years after High School. A Report from the National Longitudinal Transition Study-2 (NCSER 2011-3005)*. Menlo Park, CA: SRI International.

Nickerson, R.S. (1998) "Confirmation bias: A ubiquitous phenomenon in many guises." *Review of General Psychology 2*, 2, 175–220.

Reber, D. (2020) *Differently Wired: A Parent's Guide to Raising an Atypical Child with Confidence and Hope*. New York, NY: Workman Publishing.

Resnick, L.B. (1995) "From aptitude to effort: A new foundation for our schools." *Daedalus 124*, 4, 55–62.

Rosenthal, R. and Fode, K.L. (1963) "The effect of experimenter bias on the performance of the albino rat." *Behavioral Science 8*, 3, 183–189.

Saphier, J. (2016) *High Expectations Teaching*. Thousand Oaks, CA: Corwin.

Siegel, D.J. (2010) *Mindsight: The New Science of Personal Transformation*. New York, NY: Bantam.

Snow, J.A. (1998) *What's Really Worth Doing and How to Do It: A Book for People Who Love Someone Labeled Disabled (Possibly Yourself)*. Toronto: Inclusion Press.

Sriram, R. (2020, April 13) "The neuroscience behind productive struggle." www.edutopia.org/article/neuroscience-behind-productive-struggle

Tolle, E. (2008) *A New Earth: Awakening to Your Life's Purpose*. New York, NY: Penguin.

Turnwald, B.P., Goyer, J.P., Boles, D.Z., Silder, A., Delp, S.L., and Crum, A.J. (2019) "Learning one's genetic risk changes physiology independent of actual genetic risk." *Nature Human Behaviour 3*, 48–56.

Uvnäs-Moberg, K., Handlin, L., and Petersson, M. (2015) "Self-soothing behaviors with particular reference to oxytocin release induced by non-noxious sensory stimulation." *Frontiers in Psychology 5*, 1529. doi:10.3389/fpsyg.2014.01529

Vigdal, J.S. and Brønnick, K.K. (2022) "A systematic review of 'helicopter parenting' and its relationship with anxiety and depression." *Frontiers in Psychology 13*. doi:10.3389/fpsyg.2022.872981

Vygotsky, L.S. (1978) *Mind in society: The development of higher psychological processes*. Massachusetts: Harvard University Press.

Zukav, G. (1999) *The Seat of the Soul*. New York, NY: Simon & Schuster.